melissa's®
HATCH CHILE
COOKBOOK

Sharon Hernandez *and* Chef Ida Rodriguez

Published in the United States by World Variety Produce, Inc.

Library of Congress Control Number: 2013934925

ISBN-10:0615779913
ISBN-13:978-0-615-77991-1
UPC: 0-45255-14630-1

Distributed by:
World Variety Produce, Inc.
PO Box 514599
Los Angeles, CA 90051

To order, contact Melissa's:
800-588-0151
www.melissas.com
hotline@melissas.com

Editing & Design:
Terrace Partners

Photography:
Melissa's/World Variety
Produce, Inc.

Printed in China
10 9 8 7 6 5 4 3 2 1

melissa's®

HATCH CHILE COOKBOOK

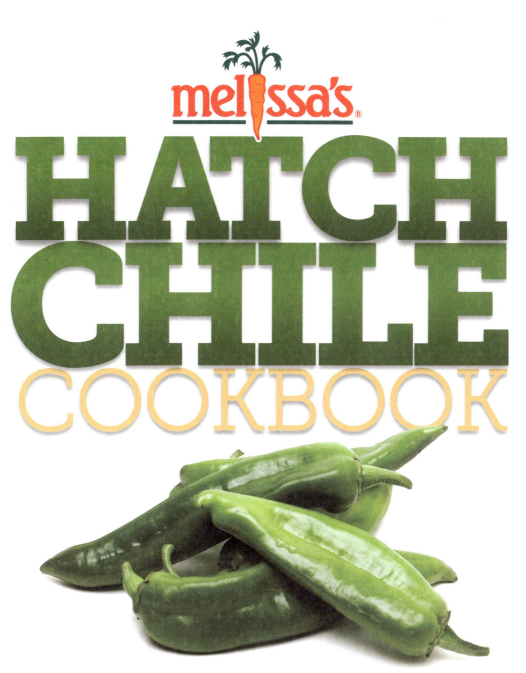

Sharon Hernandez *and* Chef Ida Rodriguez

Melissa's / World Variety Produce, Inc., is known for the freshest ideas in produce. Company founders Sharon and Joe Hernandez, along with their daughter, Melissa, have introduced exotic, conventional, and organic produce items to Food Lovers across the nation.

Melissa's / World Variety Produce leads the industry in supplying delicious and delectable tasting fruits and vegetables to supermarkets and venues all over the world. In the professional culinary world, Melissa's has long been recognized as the extraordinary supplier for the freshest and tastiest fruits and vegetables. World-renowned chefs insist upon Melissa's Produce for their signature restaurants.

Melissa's consistently shares what's in season with you, to bring the flavors of the world to your kitchen. Please visit us at www.melissas.com and be sure to look and ask for Melissa's brand in your local produce department.

HATCH CHILE

Table *of* Contents

HATCH CHILE

Introduction

Sweet childhood memories inspire so many lifelong delights, especially when it comes to food! As passionate Hatch Chile lovers, we have created this Hatch Chile cookbook to share a special selection of our favorite family recipes with you.

Fresh Hatch Chiles, grown only in the Mesilla Valley of New Mexico, are available for just a few short weeks each year, in August and September. It is a long-standing tradition in our family to end

every summer with a road trip to New Mexico to pick out our very own 50-pound burlap sack overflowing with freshly harvested green Hatch Chiles. As we drive through the valley, the savory scent of the new crop of chiles fills the air. Back at home, the mouth-watering aroma is recreated throughout the year, every time we hunger for these chiles to make our favorite Hatch Chile recipes we've collected for you here in this book.

Harvested from fertile soil along the Rio Grande, Hatch Chiles thrive in the river valley's combination of nutrient-rich soil, intense sunlight, and cool desert nights. The peppers develop thick walls and meaty, flavorful flesh unlike any other chile. Because their growing season is short, Hatch Chiles are typically bought in bulk, roasted immediately, and frozen for use throughout the year (see Hatch Chile Essentials, page 12). Nutritionally speaking, a single fresh medium-size green chile has as much Vitamin C as six oranges. Hot chile peppers are believed to burn calories by triggering a thermodynamic response in the body that speeds metabolism.

Once roasted, Hatch Chiles are easy to peel and seed. Roasting heightens the robust earthy flavor of the chiles and the texture of the thick walls of the chile pod become lusciously rich. These unique qualities, and the peppers' variable heat (unlike other chile peppers, Hatch Chiles come in varieties that cover the full spectrum of heat levels—see Hatch Chile Essentials, page 12) have earned Hatch Chiles great popularity far beyond the local community of Hatch, New Mexico, which has dubbed itself the Chile Capital of the World.

Connoisseurs and chefs from all over the globe have adopted Hatch Chiles as a condiment of choice. Many a home cook and celebrity chef have gone further, incorporating Hatch Chiles into all kinds of superb dishes from burgers, pizzas, quiches, pancakes, milkshakes, pastries, and even spiced ice cubes!

For every recipe in this book, Hatch Chiles or Hatch Chile powder (and often both) are the key ingredients. You will find a range of delicious dishes for every time of day and every occasion: breakfast, finger food, appetizers, salads, side dishes, entrees, soups, condiments,

desserts, and beverages. User friendly and palate pleasing, all of the recipes gathered here are great for any novice to sophisticated cook to prepare, for all to share, and to savor.

Happy Cooking!
Sharon Hernandez *and* Melissa's Corporate Chef Ida Rodriguez

Hatch Chile Festival in Hatch, New Mexico

HATCH CHILE

ESSENTIALS

HEAT LEVELS *and* MEASURING

Hatch Chiles come in a vast range of heat levels, from the mild end of the spicy spectrum to extremely hot. Typically, the mild to medium-hot varieties are more readily available. Any Hatch Chile variety you choose throughout the recipes in this book, mild to hot, can be personalized to your flavor preference. We recommend tasting a bit of the flesh of the Hatch Chile before proceeding with any recipe to get a taste of their heat level. We did not specify which heat level of Hatch Chile to use in our recipes. All flavors of Hatch Chile are interchangeable throughout the recipes depending on your preference.

ROASTING *and* PEELING

Hatch Chiles can be roasted over an open flame or under the broiler in an oven. The process typically takes about 8 minutes (less time for smaller chiles, more for larger).

To roast over an open flame on the stove: Use long-handled tongs to hold the chile over a medium flame, turning occasionally until evenly charred.

To roast over an open flame on a barbecue grill: This is the authentic traditional method and is the way our family prefers to roast our Hatch Chiles. Heat the grill until hot. Using long-handled tongs, turn the chiles over the direct heat until they are blackened and blistered all over.

To roast under the broiler: Preheat the broiler to high. Arrange the chiles in a single layer on a baking sheet and set under the broiler. Roast until blackened and blistered all over, turning occasionally. Once roasted, chose one of our simple methods to cool and peel:

- Transfer the roasted chiles to a paper bag and roll the top down to close the bag.

- Transfer the roasted chiles to a pan and cover with a tight-fitting lid.

- Place the roasted chiles in a bowl and cover with a damp towel or with plastic wrap.

When the chiles are cool enough to handle, peel. You will find their skin peels off easily, revealing their silky flesh underneath. If not stuffing the chiles, remove and discard stem and seeds. If you will be stuffing the chiles, leave the stem intact, cut a lengthwise slit up one side of each chile (don't cut through the tip end), and then delicately remove the seeds, being careful not to tear the chile. We recommend wearing plastic gloves when handling any chile.

STORING

Roasted Hatch Chiles can be frozen for up to 2 years
(**Note:** *Hatch Chiles become hotter over time, even when frozen!*).
Whether or not you roast your chiles in bulk, we recommend
portioning them into small resealable plastic bags before freezing. This
way you have recipe-sized amounts on-hand to defrost as needed.

Visit www.melissas.com for information about our seasonal Hatch
Chile Roasting Events, where you can purchase ready-to-go freshly
Roasted Hatch Chiles.

Happy Roasting,
Chef Ida & Sharon

BREAKFAST

Hatch Chile *and* Heirloom Tomato Frittata

makes 6 servings

12 large eggs

1 teaspoon dried oregano

1 teaspoon dried thyme

Melissa's My Grinder® Organic Garlic & Herbs with Sea Salt

Melissa's My Grinder® Organic Rainbow Peppercorns

1 tablespoon unsalted butter

2 large heirloom tomatoes, sliced

Kosher salt and freshly ground black pepper

1 cup roasted, peeled, stemmed, seeded, and chopped Hatch Chiles *(see Hatch Chile Essentials, page 12)*

8 ounces cream cheese, cubed

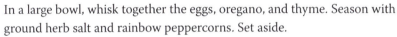

In a large bowl, whisk together the eggs, oregano, and thyme. Season with ground herb salt and rainbow peppercorns. Set aside.

In a large skillet, melt the butter over medium heat. Add the tomatoes to the pan, in batches if needed. Cook on each side for 2 minutes, or until they begin to collapse. Season with salt and pepper. Remove the tomatoes from pan and set them aside. Add the Hatch Chiles to the pan and sauté until most of the moisture in the pan has evaporated, about 1 minute. Arrange the tomatoes in a single layer on top of the chiles in the skillet and pour in the egg mixture. Scatter the cubes of cream cheese over the top. Cover the skillet and reduce the heat to low. Cook for 40 to 45 minutes or until set.

Note: *For more pungent flavor, substitute good-quality crumbled bleu cheese for the cream cheese.*

Bob's Sweet 'n Spicy Hatch Chile Pancakes

Makes 9 (6-inch) pancakes

2 cups all-purpose flour

2 teaspoons baking powder

1 teaspoon baking soda

½ teaspoon salt

3 tablespoons granulated sugar

2 large eggs, lightly beaten

3 cups buttermilk

4 tablespoons (½ stick) unsalted butter, melted

½ cup roasted, peeled, stemmed, seeded, and chopped Hatch Chiles *(see Hatch Chile Essentials, page 12)*

Cooking spray

Melissa's Organic Blue Agave Syrup, for serving

Preheat the oven to 175°F. Heat a nonstick griddle to 375°F over medium-high heat.

Whisk together the flour, baking powder, baking soda, salt, and sugar in a medium bowl. Add the eggs, buttermilk, melted butter, and Hatch Chiles. Whisk to combine.

Lightly coat a griddle or large skillet with cooking spray. Ladle ½ cupfuls of the batter onto the griddle. When bubbles form on the surface of the pancakes and they are slightly dry around the edges (about 2½ minutes), flip them over. Cook until golden on the bottom, about 1 minute more. Hold the finished pancakes on a heatproof plate in the oven while making remaining pancakes. Serve warm.

Note: *For added spice, add one whole roasted and peeled hot Hatch Chile to a bottle of Melissa's Organic Blue Agave Syrup. Refrigerate the chile syrup at least 8 hours before using. It also makes a great dressing for fruit salad.*

Green Chile Chilaquiles

makes 4 servings

Corn oil

1 dozen corn tortillas, quartered

Salt

2 cups Tomatillo and Hatch Chile
Verde Sauce *(page 152)*

Cotija cheese or queso fresco,
for garnish

Crema Mexicana, crème fraîche,
or sour cream, for garnish

Chopped cilantro, for garnish

Chopped red onion, for garnish

Sliced or chopped avocado,
for garnish

4 to 8 fried eggs, for serving

Set a large sauté pan over medium-high heat, add corn oil to a depth of
1 inch, and heat the oil to 350°F. Working in batches and adding oil as needed
to maintain 1 inch in the pan, fry the tortilla quarters until golden brown,
about 1 minute or less. Transfer the fried tortillas to a paper towel-lined
plate to soak up excess oil. Sprinkle a little salt on the tortillas.

Remove the pan from the heat and wipe it clean. Add 2 tablespoons of corn
oil to the pan and heat over high heat. Add the tomatillo sauce and cook for
several minutes, stirring frequently. Add the fried tortilla quarters to the sauce
and gently turn the pieces of tortilla until they are all well coated with sauce.
Let cook for a few minutes more to heat through. Garnish the chilaquiles
with cheese, crema, cilantro, onion, and avocado; serve with fried eggs.

Hatch *and* Farro Breakfast Patties

makes 8 to 10 servings

1 (6-ounce) package Melissa's Organic Farro

1 pound Melissa's Baby Dutch Yellow® Potatoes, halved

Sea salt

4 tablespoons (½ stick) unsalted butter, divided

4 tablespoons extra-virgin olive oil, divided

2 Melissa's Perfect Sweet Onions, thinly sliced

Freshly ground black pepper

3 Hatch Chiles, roasted, peeled, stemmed, seeded, and chopped
(see Hatch Chile Essentials, page 12)

1 pound fresh button mushrooms, chopped

3 cloves garlic, minced

1 tablespoon smoked paprika

1 tablespoon Melissa's My Grinder® Organic Italian Seasoning

1 teaspoon Melissa's Hatch Chile Powder

2 tablespoons dry sherry

¼ cup finely chopped fresh chives

1 cup panko breadcrumbs

1 cup shredded Gruyère cheese

2 large eggs

Canola oil, for frying

Prepare the farro according to the package instructions. Set aside to cool briefly.

Place the potatoes in a pot and cover with cold water. Add salt to taste, bring to a boil, and cook until the potatoes are fork-tender, about 10 minutes. Drain the potatoes and transfer them to a large bowl. Mash the potatoes and set aside to cool briefly.

Heat 2 tablespoons of the olive oil and 2 tablespoons of the butter in a sauté pan. Add the onions, season with salt and pepper, and sauté until they are softened and lightly browned, 5 to 7 minutes. Add the onions to the potatoes.

continued

Hatch and Farro Breakfast Patties continued

Heat the remaining 2 tablespoons of olive oil and 2 tablespoons of butter in the sauté pan. Add the Hatch Chiles, mushrooms, garlic, smoked paprika, Italian seasoning, and Hatch Chile powder. Cook the mixture until the mushrooms are tender, about 5 minutes, and then add the sherry. Sauté until most of the moisture is evaporated. Add to the potatoes.

Add the chives, breadcrumbs, cheese, eggs, and cooked farro to the potato mixture. Use your hands to mix until thoroughly combined. Form into 8 to 10 patties about ¼-inch thick.

Wipe the sauté pan clean, set it over medium heat, add canola oil to a depth of about ½ inch, and heat until the oil shimmers. Fry the patties until golden brown on each side, turning once, about 3 minutes per side.

Green Chile Omelet

makes 1 omelet

Cooking spray

2 large eggs

2 tablespoons whole milk

¼ teaspoon salt

1 pinch black pepper

⅓ cup shredded low-fat pepper Jack cheese

1 Hatch Chile, roasted, peeled, stemmed, seeded, and chopped
(see Hatch Chile Essentials, page 12)

2 tablespoons sour cream

2 tablespoons chopped tomatoes

¼ avocado, sliced

Lightly coat an 8-inch nonstick skillet with cooking spray, then preheat over medium-high heat.

In a mixing bowl, whisk together the eggs, milk, salt, and pepper until blended, then pour the mixture into the pan. As the omelet cooks, gently lift the edges with a spatula to allow uncooked egg mixture to run underneath. When the egg mixture is no longer runny but still wet, use the spatula to loosen the edges of the omelet and flip it over. Quickly sprinkle on the cheese and chiles, fold the omelet in half over the fillings, and turn the omelet out onto a warm plate. Top with sour cream, tomatoes, and avocado. Serve hot.

Make-Ahead Breakfast Enchiladas

makes 12 servings

Vegetable oil or unsalted butter

10 corn tortillas

2 cups diced cooked ham

½ cup chopped green onions

4 Hatch Chiles, roasted, peeled, stemmed, seeded, and chopped *(see Hatch Chile Essentials, page 12)*

2 cups shredded cheddar cheese, divided

6 large eggs

2 cups 1% milk

½ teaspoon salt

¼ teaspoon Melissa's Hatch Chile Powder

Grease a 13 by 9-inch baking dish.

Lay out the tortillas on a work surface and evenly layer into the center of each tortilla the ham, onions, chiles, and 1¼ cups of the cheese. Roll up the tortillas and set them seam-side down in the prepared baking dish. Whisk together the eggs, milk, salt, and chile powder. Pour the egg mixture evenly over the tortillas. Cover and chill overnight, or at least 8 hours.

Remove the baking dish from the refrigerator and let stand 30 minutes at room temperature before baking.

Preheat the oven to 350°F.

Cover the baking dish with foil and bake for 20 minutes. Remove the foil and bake 15 more minutes. Sprinkle on the remaining ¾ cup of cheese and bake until the cheese melts, 3 to 4 more minutes. Let stand 10 minutes before serving.

Huevos Rancheros

makes 2 to 4 servings

1 teaspoon olive oil

4 corn tortillas

2 teaspoons unsalted butter

4 large eggs

2 cups Melissa's Hatch Salsa Ranchera *(page 157)*

2 tablespoons fresh chopped cilantro *(optional)*

Preheat the oven to 200°F. Heat the olive oil in a large nonstick skillet on medium-high, turning the pan to coat it with the oil. One by one, heat the tortillas in the pan for 1 to 2 minutes per side, until heated through and softened. Immediately transfer each warm tortilla to a plate in the oven to keep warm while you cook the rest of the tortillas and the eggs.

To fry the eggs, keep the skillet over medium-high heat. Add the butter to the pan. When the butter has melted, crack the eggs into the skillet and cook for 3 to 4 minutes for runny yolks, or slightly longer for firmer yolks.

To serve, spoon ½ cup of the salsa onto each of 4 warmed plates. Top with a warm tortilla, then a fried egg. Top with more sauce and a sprinkle of cilantro.

Hatch Breakfast Burrito

makes 4 servings

1 pound breakfast sausage

½ Melissa's Perfect Sweet Onion, finely diced

1 Melissa's Fire-Roasted Sweet Bell Pepper, chopped

2 Hatch Chiles, roasted, peeled, stemmed, seeded, and chopped *(see Hatch Chile Essentials, page 12)*

1 Roma tomato, finely diced

8 large eggs, beaten

4 large (10-inch) flour tortillas, warmed

Heat a large skillet over medium heat. Crumble and brown the sausage in the skillet. Transfer the cooked sausage to a paper towel-lined dish to drain. Pour off all but 2 tablespoons of the sausage drippings from the pan, then raise the heat to medium-high and sauté the onion and bell peppers until they begin to soften, about 5 minutes. Stir in the chiles and the tomatoes and continue cooking for 5 more minutes. Add the eggs and the sausage to the pan and stir to mix. Continue cooking, stirring almost constantly, until the eggs begin to set, 2 to 3 minutes.

Divide the egg mixture among the 4 tortillas; roll and serve.

Note: *Try substituting sweet Italian sausage for the breakfast sausage; the sweetness pairs well with the spiciness of the chile.*

Potato *and* Hatch Croquettes

makes 15 croquettes

2 pounds Melissa's Baby Dutch Yellow® Potatoes

4 teaspoons salt, divided

2 tablespoons whole milk

1 teaspoon Melissa's Hatch Chile Powder

3 Hatch Chiles, roasted, peeled, stemmed, seeded, and chopped *(see Hatch Chile Essentials, page 12)*

2 large egg yolks, beaten

3 tablespoons all-purpose flour

1 large egg, beaten

Dried breadcrumbs, sifted

Vegetable oil, for frying

Put the potatoes in a pot and cover with cold water. Season with 2 teaspoons of the salt, bring to a boil, and cook until the potatoes are fork-tender, about 10 minutes. Drain the potatoes and set aside to cool briefly.

In a large bowl, combine the milk, chile powder, chiles, egg yolks, and flour. Mash the potatoes and add them to the bowl. Season the mixture with 1 to 2 teaspoons salt and mix well. Cover and refrigerate until thoroughly chilled.

Shape the potato mixture into 15 small oblong croquettes. Dip each croquette in the beaten egg, then roll through the breadcrumbs.

Set a large saucepan or Dutch oven over medium heat, add oil to a depth of ½ inch, and heat the oil to 350°F.

Working in small batches, fry the croquettes until brown on all sides, 3 to 5 minutes. Drain on a paper towel-lined plate. Serve hot.

Corn *and* Green Chile Quiche

~~~ *makes 1 (9-inch) quiche* ~~~

1 (9-inch) prebaked pie crust

3 eggs

1 cup whole milk

½ cup heavy cream

2 cups shredded pepper Jack cheese

1 cup corn kernels

3 Hatch Chiles, roasted, peeled, stemmed, seeded, and chopped
(see Hatch Chile Essentials, page 12)

½ teaspoon salt

Cracked black pepper

1 teaspoon Melissa's Hatch Chile Powder

2 green onions, sliced

Preheat the oven to 350°F.

In a large bowl, combine the eggs, milk, and cream. Whisk until uniform. Add the cheese, corn, chiles, salt, pepper, and chile powder. Stir to evenly combine. Pour the mixture into the prebaked pie crust.

Sprinkle green onions over the top of the quiche. Bake 40 to 50 minutes or until the filling is puffed, set, and starting to brown. Cool before serving.

Papas con Chile

~~~ *makes 6 servings* ~~~

2 pounds Melissa's Baby Dutch Yellow® Potatoes, peeled and cut into ½-inch dice

Salt

½ cup whole milk

2 tablespoons unsalted butter

1 cup shredded cheddar cheese

4 Hatch Chiles, roasted, peeled, stemmed, seeded, and chopped
(see Hatch Chile Essentials, page 12)

Put the potatoes in a pot and cover with cold water. Add salt to taste, bring to a boil, and cook until the potatoes are fork-tender, about 10 minutes. Drain the potatoes and return them to the pot.

Heat the milk in a small saucepan over low heat. Add the cheese and butter, whisking until the mixture is smooth.

Mash the potatoes with potato masher or large fork; add the milk and cheese mixture and stir in the chiles. Mix until the potatoes are smooth. Season to taste with salt and serve hot.

Sausage *and* Hatch Brunch Casserole

makes 6 servings

Vegetable oil or cooking spray

1 pound breakfast sausage

1 (15-ounce) carton Egg Beaters® Southwestern Style

2 cups whole milk

1 teaspoon salt

1 teaspoon garlic powder

1 cup roasted, peeled, stemmed, seeded, and chopped Hatch Chiles
(see Hatch Chile Essentials, page 12)

2 slices bread, cubed

1 cup shredded sharp cheddar cheese

Preheat a large skillet over medium heat. Lightly grease a 9 by 13-inch baking dish.

Cook the sausage in the skillet, crumbling it as it cooks, until it is browned. Drain off and discard the drippings.

In a bowl, whisk together the Egg Beaters®, milk, salt, and garlic powder. Stir in the chiles.

Layer the bread cubes, sausage, and cheese in the baking dish. Pour the egg mixture into the baking, pressing the bread down with a spoon to saturate it completely. Cover and refrigerate overnight, or at least 8 hours.

Preheat the oven to 350°F. Take the casserole out of the refrigerator and let sit about 1 hour to come to room temperature.

Bake the casserole for 45 minutes, or until the cheese is bubbly and the filling is firm.

APPETIZERS

Hatch Chile Guacamole

Melissa's Hatch Chile Pinwheels

makes 16 appetizer servings

8 ounces cream cheese, softened

½ teaspoon garlic powder

⅓ cup roasted, peeled, seeded, and chopped Hatch Chiles
(see Hatch Chile Essentials, page 12)

4 (10-inch) flour tortillas

Melissa's Hatch Chile Powder

Combine the cream cheese and garlic powder in a small bowl, stirring until well blended. Mix in the chiles.

Divide the cheese mixture among the four tortillas, spreading evenly. Roll the tortillas up tightly. Refrigerate until firm, about 1 hour.

Cut each roll crosswise into 4 (1-inch thick) rounds. Arrange the pinwheels on a serving platter, sprinkle with Hatch Chile powder, and serve.

Hatch Chile Guacamole

makes about 5 cups

4 ripe avocados

2 Hatch Chiles, roasted, peeled, stemmed, seeded, and chopped
(see Hatch Chile Essentials, page 12)

½ white onion, finely chopped

2 tablespoons freshly squeezed lemon juice

½ cup finely chopped fresh cilantro

1 teaspoon salt

Tortilla Chips, for serving

Peel and pit the avocados. Mash the avocados in a large bowl with a fork until almost smooth. Fold in the chiles, onions, lemon juice, cilantro, and salt. Taste and add more salt if desired.

Serve with your favorite tortilla chips or make your own Homemade Spicy Chips (page 32).

Homemade Spicy Chips

makes 48 chips

6 corn tortillas

Olive oil, for brushing

Melissa's Hatch Chile Powder

Preheat the oven to 350°F.

Lightly brush the tortillas with olive oil on both sides, then sprinkle with Hatch Chile powder—sparingly for mild flavor, generously for spicier chips. Cut each tortilla into 8 wedges and spread in a single layer on a baking sheet, spacing at least ¼ inch apart.

Bake the tortilla wedges for 8 minutes, then check every 1 to 2 minutes, watching carefully for the moment when the chips start to turn crispy and slightly golden brown at the edges. Cool before serving.

Variations

Spice: *Combine one of these with the Hatch Chile powder and sprinkle on the chips before baking: paprika, cumin, onion powder, or garlic powder (sparingly).*

Cheese: *Combine grated Parmesan, cheddar, or pepper Jack cheese with the Hatch Chile powder and sprinkle on the chips before baking.*

Sweet: *Mix cinnamon-sugar with the Hatch Chile powder and sprinkle on the chips before baking.*

Black Bean Layered Dip

makes 4 to 5 cups

1 (8-ounce) package cream cheese, softened

1 cup cooked black beans, rinsed and drained

1 (14.5-ounce) can diced tomatoes, drained

2 Hatch Chiles, roasted, peeled, stemmed, seeded, and chopped
(see Hatch Chile Essentials, page 12)

1 cup finely shredded cheddar cheese

Spread the cream cheese in an even layer across the bottom of shallow dish, such as a pie plate. Layer on the beans, tomatoes, chiles, and cheese. Serve at room temperature with chips.

Mushroom and Hatch Dip

makes 4 to 5 cups

1 cup sautéed chopped mushrooms

1 (10-ounce) package frozen chopped spinach, thawed, and well drained

4 Hatch Chiles, roasted, peeled, stemmed, seeded, and chopped
(see Hatch Chile Essentials, page 12)

¾ cup grated Parmesan cheese

¾ cup mayonnaise

½ cup shredded mozzarella cheese

½ teaspoon Melissa's Hatch Chile Powder

Crackers or crudités, for serving

Preheat the oven to 350°F. Lightly grease a 9-inch quiche dish or pie plate.

Combine the mushrooms, spinach, chiles, Parmesan, mayonnaise, mozzarella, and chile powder in a bowl. Mix well. Spoon the mixture into the prepared dish. Bake until set, about 20 minutes.

Serve with crackers or assorted fresh vegetable crudités.

Oven-Baked Soft Pretzels
with Hatch Chile Mustard

makes 12 to 14 pretzels

5 teaspoons active dry yeast

2 cups warm water

¼ cup whole milk, warmed

2 tablespoons brown sugar

10 tablespoons unsalted butter, melted, divided

1 tablespoon Melissa's Hatch Chile Powder

5 teaspoons sea salt, divided

6 cups all-purpose flour

Canola oil

Cornmeal, for baking sheets

6 quarts water

¾ cup baking soda

2 Hatch Chiles, roasted, peeled, stemmed, seeded, and minced *(see Hatch Chile Essentials, page 12)*

½ cups whole-grain mustard

Combine the yeast, warm water, milk, brown sugar, and 6 tablespoons of the melted butter in a bowl. Whisk until the ingredients are combined and the yeast and sugar are dissolved. Set aside to rest in a warm place for 10 to 15 minutes.

Pour the yeast mixture into the bowl of a stand mixer fitted with a dough hook. Blend the mixture at medium-low speed and, with the machine running, add the chile powder and 2 teaspoons of the salt. Gradually add the flour and continue mixing until the dough forms a ball. (It should be somewhat tacky.) Remove the bowl from the mixer. Take the dough out of the bowl and set it aside. Add a little canola oil to the bowl (1 to 2 teaspoons should be enough). Return the dough ball to the bowl and roll to coat it with the oil. Cover and set in a warm area to rest for 30 minutes.

Return the bowl to the mixer fitted with the dough hook and mix for 5 minutes. Remove the bowl from the mixer, cover, and let rise in a warm area for 1 hour.

Preheat the oven to 400°F. Spread two baking sheets with a thin layer of cornmeal.

In a large pot, bring the water to a boil.

Punch down the dough. Separate it into 12 to 14 baseball-size portions. Use your hands to roll each ball into a rope about 1 inch thick and 10 inches

continued

Oven-Baked Soft Pretzels continued

long. Shape into a circle, overlapping the ends by about 4 inches. Taking one end of dough in each hand, twist at the point where the dough overlaps. Carefully lift each end across to the opposite edge of the circle. Press the ends firmly to attach.

When the water boils, slowly add the baking soda, being careful as it will bubble up. Working in batches, add the pretzels, one at a time, and cook for 30 seconds, turning to cook evenly. Set the boiled the pretzels on the prepared baking sheets.

Sprinkle the boiled pretzels with the remaining 3 teaspoons of sea salt. Bake for 22 minutes, rotating the baking sheets halfway through the baking time. Remove the pretzels from the oven, brush with the remaining 4 tablespoons of melted butter and let cool.

For the mustard spread, combine the chiles and mustard in a small bowl and mix thoroughly.

Serve the pretzels warm or at room temperature, with the chile mustard.

Red Quinoa Cheese Puffs
with Hatch Chile Jelly

makes 2½ dozen puffs

1 cup Melissa's Organic Red Quinoa

4 ounces (1 stick) unsalted butter, melted and cooled

2 large eggs

1¾ cups whole milk

1 cup cornmeal

2 teaspoons baking powder

Sea salt and freshly ground black pepper

¼ cup roasted, peeled, stemmed, seeded, and chopped Hatch Chiles *(see Hatch Chile Essentials, page 12)*

2 red apples, peeled, cored, and finely diced

½ cup rehydrated Melissa's Roasted Sweet Corn *(see Note below)*

1 cup shredded cheddar cheese

1 cup shredded Gruyère cheese

Hatch Chile Jelly *(page 148)*

Use a blender on high speed to pulverize the quinoa to a powder. Set aside.

Preheat the oven to 425°F. Lightly grease a mini muffin tin.

In a bowl, whisk together the butter, eggs, and milk until well combined. In another bowl, combine the pulverized quinoa with the cornmeal and baking powder and mix well. Season the dry ingredients with salt and pepper, add to the wet ingredients, and mix to combine. Stir in the chiles, apples, corn, and the cheeses.

Spoon the batter into the muffin tin. Bake for 12 to 15 minutes, or until a toothpick inserted into the center comes out clean.

To serve, arrange the puffs on a platter and top each with a dab of the jelly.

Note: *To rehydrate the roasted sweet corn, put it in a heatproof bowl, add hot water to cover by 2 inches, and leave to soak until tender, about 20 minutes. Drain thoroughly before using.*

Meaty-Cheesy Bread *with* Hatch Chiles

makes 6 to 8 servings

1 (1-pound) package prepared pizza dough, such as Trader Joe's, at room temperature

2 tablespoons vegetable or olive oil, plus more as needed

½ Melissa's Perfect Sweet Onion, thinly sliced

⅛ to ¼ teaspoon granulated garlic

½ cup shredded cheddar cheese

½ cup shredded Jack cheese

2 links sweet Italian sausage, casings removed

1 (3-ounce) package sliced pepperoni

1½ bell peppers (a combination of green, yellow, and red), thinly sliced

3 Hatch Chiles, roasted, peeled, stemmed, seeded, and chopped *(see Hatch Chile Essentials, page 12)*

Preheat the oven to 450°F. Lightly oil a large baking sheet.

Caramelize the onions by sautéing them for about 15 minutes in the olive oil in a skillet over medium heat, stirring occasionally but not frequently. The onions will begin to soften, then start to turn a little brown. As they darken, stir more frequently to prevent burning. When the onions are almost brown and have an intense, rich flavor, they're caramelized. The process can take at least 25 minutes.

Stretch the dough into a 12-inch circle and set it on the prepared baking sheet. Sprinkle the dough with the granulated garlic and bake it in the oven for 15 minutes or until the dough is golden brown.

Remove the dough from the oven and sprinkle with the cheeses, then layer on the sausage, pepperoni, onions, bell peppers, and Hatch Chiles.

Return the bread to the oven and bake until the cheese is melted, about 5 minutes. Serve hot.

Note: *This bread is great with marinara dipping sauce.*

Frittata-Stuffed Portobello Mushroom Caps

makes 8 servings

Oil or cooking spray

12 large eggs

Melissa's My Grinder® Organic Italian Seasoning

Melissa's My Grinder® Organic Rainbow Peppercorns

1 tablespoon unsalted butter

1 large heirloom tomato, top and bottom removed, thickly sliced into 4 rounds

Salt and freshly ground black pepper

10 fresh basil leaves, cut into ribbons *(see Note, page 78)*

2 Hatch Chiles, roasted, peeled, stemmed, seeded, and chopped *(see Hatch Chile Essentials, page 12)*

4 large Portobello mushrooms, stems and gills removed *(see Note below)*

4 ounces cream cheese, cubed

Preheat the oven to 350°F. Lightly oil a baking dish.

In a large bowl, whisk together the eggs and a few grindings of the Italian seasoning and rainbow peppercorns. Set aside.

In a large skillet, melt the butter over medium heat and cook the tomatoes, turning once, just until the tomatoes release their moisture, about 1 to 2 minutes. Season to taste with salt and pepper, then add the basil and chiles and continue cooking just until the basil begins to wilt, about 1 minute.

To stuff the Portobellos, fit 1 tomato slice into each mushroom cap and one-fourth of the basil and chiles. Pour in egg mixture to nearly fill the mushroom. Top each Portobello with a few cubes of cream cheese.

Bake the stuffed mushrooms in the prepared baking dish for 35 to 45 minutes, or until the filling is set.

Note: *Gently scooping out some of the meat of the mushroom cap often helps the stuffing fit nicely.*

Wings *with* Hatch Dipping Sauce

makes 6 servings

Cooking spray

36 chicken drumettes

Sea salt and freshly ground black pepper

1 cup sour cream

¼ cup chicken broth

2 Hatch Chiles, roasted, peeled, stemmed, and seeded
(see Hatch Chile Essentials, page 12)

Preheat the oven to 350°F. Lightly coat 2 large baking sheets with cooking spray.

Put the chicken drumettes in a large pot, cover with cold water, and bring the water to a gentle boil over medium-high heat. Cook for 15 minutes, lowering the heat as needed to keep the water at a steady but gentle boil.

Drain the drumettes and pat them dry with paper towels. Transfer the drumettes to the prepared baking sheets. Season with salt and pepper and bake until the meat begins to pull away from the bone and is no longer pink, about 10 minutes. (You can double-check for doneness with a meat thermometer, which should read 170°F when inserted in the meatiest part of the drumette.)

While the drumettes are cooking, make the dipping sauce: combine the sour cream, chicken broth, Hatch Chiles, and a pinch of salt in a blender and mix until smooth. Pour the sauce into a bowl and set aside.

Arrange the drumettes on a platter and serve with the sauce.

Flash-Fried Pizza Nibbles

makes about 36 mini pizzas

DOUGH

1 cup warm water

1 tablespoon honey

2½ teaspoons active dry yeast

2½ cups all-purpose flour

½ teaspoon sea salt

2 teaspoons Melissa's My Grinder® Organic Italian Seasoning

2 tablespoons extra-virgin olive oil

Canola oil, for frying

TOPPING

1 cup shredded mozzarella cheese

1 (24-ounce) jar pasta sauce

2 cups sliced button mushrooms, sautéed, cooled, and chopped

5 Hatch Chiles, roasted, peeled, stemmed, seeded, and chopped *(see Hatch Chile Essentials, page 12)*

1 (9.5-ounce) jar Melissa's Pimientos Del Piquillo, drained and chopped

2 (14.75-ounce) jars marinated artichoke hearts, drained and chopped

In a small bowl, mix together the warm water and honey. Stir in the yeast, then set aside in a warm place and let stand for 15 minutes.

In the bowl of a stand mixer, whisk together the flour, salt, and Italian seasoning. Attach a dough hook to the mixer. With the mixer on medium speed, gradually add the yeast mixture to the flour mixture. Keep the mixer running until the dough is smooth and firm, 5 to 6 minutes.

Remove the bowl from the mixer. Drizzle the olive oil onto the dough and turn it a few times with your hands to completely coat with the oil. Cover the dough in the bowl and set in a warm place to rise until the dough has doubled in size, about 20 minutes.

Turn the dough out onto a lightly floured surface and roll it out to about ⅛ inch thick. Using a 3-inch biscuit cutter, cut the dough into about 36 rounds.

Set a large deep skillet over medium-high heat, add canola oil to a depth of about 1 inch, and heat the oil to 375°F. Working in batches, carefully fry the dough in the hot oil. The dough will cook in seconds. Use a slotted spoon to

continued

Flash-Fried Pizza Nibbles continued

lift the rounds out of the oil as soon as they turn golden brown. Drain on paper towels, gently pressing with a spoon to flatten any rounds that have puffed up.

Preheat the oven (and a baking stone if you have one) to 350°F. Lightly oil 2 large baking sheets.

To assemble the pizza nibbles, top the rounds with the cheese, then add some sauce, followed by mushrooms, chiles, pimientos, and artichoke hearts. Arrange the pizzas on baking sheets and bake for 5 to 8 minutes, or until the cheese melts and the nibbles are heated through. Serve hot.

Note: *Layering the cheese onto the dough before the other toppings helps prevent the dough from absorbing moisture and getting soggy.*

Shrimp *and* Hatch Chile Jalapeño Poppers

~~~ *makes 8 to 10 servings* ~~~

Vegetable oil or cooking spray

½ pound peeled, deveined fresh shrimp

Sea salt and freshly ground black pepper

3 Hatch Chiles, roasted, peeled, stemmed, seeded, and chopped
(see Hatch Chile Essentials, page 12)

4 cups shredded sharp cheddar cheese

16 large jalapeño peppers

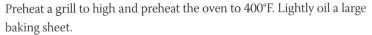

Preheat a grill to high and preheat the oven to 400°F. Lightly oil a large baking sheet.

Rinse the shrimp and pat them dry with paper towels. Set the shrimp on the hot grill, season them with salt and pepper, and cook until opaque, 1 to 2 minutes per side. Let cool.

Chop the shrimp into small pieces. In a bowl, combine the shrimp, Hatch Chiles, and cheese, mixing well.

To stuff the jalapeños, make a lengthwise slit in each one (don't cut through the tip) and carefully remove the seeds and ribs. Use a small spoon to fill each pepper with the shrimp mixture. Arrange the stuffed peppers on the prepared baking sheet. Bake 7 to 10 minutes, or until the jalapeños are tender and the cheese has melted. Serve hot.

Note: *Refrigerate any leftover shrimp stuffing. It makes a great dip for crackers or crostini.*

Seven Layer Dip

makes 6 to 8 servings

1 pound lean ground beef

2 tablespoons Melissa's Hatch Chile Powder

1 (16-ounce) can refried beans

8 ounces sour cream

3 tomatoes, diced

1 cup prepared mild salsa

3 Hatch Chiles, roasted, peeled, stemmed, seeded, and chopped *(see Hatch Chile Essentials, page 12)*

1½ cups shredded cheese, such as Mexican blend

Tortilla chips, for serving

Brown the beef in a nonstick skillet over medium-high heat. Drain off the rendered fat, then season the meat with the chile powder and set it aside to cool.

In an 8 by 8-inch square dish, spread the refried beans in an even layer, followed by the ground beef, then the sour cream, tomatoes, salsa, and Hatch Chiles. Top with the shredded cheese. Chill at least 2 hours before serving. Serve with tortilla chips.

Southwest Eggrolls

makes 6 eggrolls

1 tablespoon vegetable oil

2 tablespoons minced green onion

2 tablespoons diced red bell pepper

⅓ cup corn kernels

¼ cup cooked black beans, rinsed and drained

2 Hatch Chiles, roasted, peeled, stemmed, seeded, and chopped
(see Hatch Chile Essentials, page 12)

½ teaspoon ground cumin

½ teaspoon Melissa's Hatch Chile Powder

⅓ teaspoon salt

¾ cup shredded Jack cheese

6 Melissa's Won Ton Wraps

1 quart canola oil, for deep-frying

Heat the vegetable oil in a medium saucepan over medium heat. Add the green onions and bell peppers. Sauté the mixture for 5 minutes, or until tender. Mix in the corn, black beans, Hatch Chiles, cumin, chile powder, and salt. Cook, stirring, for 5 minutes, until well blended and heated through. Remove the pan from the heat, add the cheese, and stir until it is melted and combined.

Use a spoon to divide the filling among the wrappers. Fold in the ends of each wrapper, then roll tightly closed.

In a large deep pot over medium-high heat, heat the oil to 375°F. Deep-fry the eggrolls until they are dark golden brown. Drain on paper towels before serving.

Honey Mustard Pretzel Crunch

makes 6 to 8 servings

Oil or cooking spray

4 ounces (1 stick) unsalted butter

½ cup honey

2 (12-ounce) packages pretzel pieces (honey mustard and

onion flavor), such as Snyder's of Hanover

3 (6-ounce) cans smoked almonds

2 tablespoons Melissa's Hatch Chile Powder

Preheat the oven to 350°F. Lightly coat 2 large baking sheets with oil or cooking spray.

In a small microwave-safe bowl, combine the butter and honey, then cover and heat in a microwave on medium-high until melted. Stir to blend.

In a large bowl, combine the pretzels, almonds, and Hatch Chile powder. Add the butter and honey mixture and mix well. Spread the pretzels in a single layer on the baking sheets. Bake for 15 minutes.

Let the mixture cool, then transfer to a serving bowl, toss, and serve.

Note: *Pair with ice-cold beer for a great cocktail snack.*

Hatch Chile Cornbread

makes 8 to 10 pieces

Vegetable oil or cooking spray

1 cup all-purpose flour

¾ cup cornmeal

3 tablespoons granulated sugar

2½ teaspoons baking powder

¾ teaspoon salt

2 large eggs, beaten

1 cup whole milk

¼ cup vegetable oil or melted unsalted butter

½ cup shredded cheddar cheese

½ cup roasted, peeled, stemmed, seeded, and chopped Hatch Chiles
(see Hatch Chile Essentials, page 12)

Preheat the oven to 400°F. Grease a square (9 by 9 by 1½-inch or 8 by 8 by 2-inch) baking pan.

In a large bowl, whisk together the flour, cornmeal, sugar, baking powder, and salt. In a separate bowl, combine the eggs, milk, and oil. Add the egg mixture all at once to the flour mixture. Stir just until moistened (do not overmix). Fold in the cheese and the chiles. Pour the batter into the prepared pan and bake for 15 to 20 minutes, or until a wooden toothpick inserted in the center comes out clean.

Let the cornbread cool slightly before cutting it into wedges or squares. Serve warm.

Hatch Chile con Queso

makes 3 cups

1 tablespoon vegetable oil

1 onion, finely chopped

1 tomato, chopped

1 jalapeño chile, minced

8 Hatch Chiles, roasted, peeled, stemmed, seeded,

and chopped *(see Hatch Chile Essentials, page 12)*

1 pound VELVEETA®, cubed

½ cup whole milk, plus more as needed

Chips, crackers, or vegetables, for serving

In a large skillet over medium-high heat, heat the oil until shimmering. Sauté the onions, tomatoes, and the jalapeño and Hatch Chiles until the onions are translucent and soft. Lower the heat to low and add the cheese, stirring constantly until completely melted. Add the milk and mix well, adding more as needed for desired consistency.

Cool slightly before serving. Serve with chips, crackers, or vegetables.

Hatch Chile Corn Muffins

makes 12 muffins

Cooking spray

1 cup all-purpose flour

1 cup yellow cornmeal

2 tablespoons granulated sugar

4 teaspoons baking powder

1 teaspoon salt

1 cup buttermilk

¼ cup vegetable oil

2 eggs, lightly beaten

½ cup shredded cheddar cheese

¼ cup roasted, peeled, stemmed, seeded, and chopped Hatch Chiles *(see Hatch Chile Essentials, page 12)*

Preheat the oven to 425°F. Lightly coat a 12-cup muffin tin with cooking spray.

In a medium bowl, whisk together the flour, cornmeal, sugar, baking powder, and salt. In a separate bowl, stir together the buttermilk, oil, and eggs. Add the wet ingredients to the dry ingredients. Stir just enough to combine (do not overmix). Fold in the cheese and chiles.

Spoon the batter into the prepared muffin cups. Bake for 22 to 25 minutes, or until a wooden toothpick comes out clean. Serve warm.

Crab-Stuffed Veggie Sweet Mini Peppers

makes about 12 stuffed peppers

1 pound Melissa's Veggie Sweet Mini Peppers, stems, tops, and seeds removed

1 ripe avocado

½ lemon

12 ounces cream cheese, softened

¼ cup sour cream

1 cup crabmeat

2 Hatch Chiles, roasted, peeled, stemmed, seeded, and chopped *(see Hatch Chile Essentials, page 12)*

Slice and pit the avocado. Scoop the avocado into a medium bowl, and squeeze the lemon over it. Mash the avocado with a potato masher or large fork. Mix in the cream cheese and sour cream. Add the crab and the chiles, then mix until well combined. Use a small spoon to fill the mini peppers with the stuffing. Serve immediately.

Hatch Chile Deviled Eggs

makes 2 dozen deviled eggs

12 large eggs

½ cup mayonnaise

1 teaspoon dry mustard

2 tablespoons sweet pickle relish

Salt and freshly ground black pepper

2 teaspoons Melissa's Hatch Chile Powder

In a large pot, combine the eggs with enough cold water to cover by 1 inch. Set the pot over high heat and bring the water to a boil. When the water comes to a boil, remove the pot from the heat, then cover and let sit for 17 minutes.

Transfer the eggs to a bowl of ice water. When they are cool enough to handle, carefully peel the eggs and rinse them. Slice each egg in half lengthwise. Remove the yolks and transfer them to a mixing bowl. Reserve the whites.

Mash the yolks with a fork. Add the mayonnaise, mustard, and relish. Season the mixture with salt and pepper. Mix until creamy.

Pipe or scoop the yolk mixture into the reserved egg white halves. Arrange on a platter or serving dish and sprinkle with Hatch Chile powder. Keep refrigerated until ready to serve, up to 24 hours.

Hatch Chile Grilled Quesadilla

makes 2 large quesadillas (4 to 6 appetizer-size portions)

4 large (10-inch) flour tortillas

3 cups shredded cheddar or Jack cheese

3 Hatch Chiles, roasted, peeled, stemmed, seeded, and diced
(see Hatch Chile Essentials, page 12)

Salsa, for serving

Preheat a grill or broiler to high heat. Lay 1 tortilla on a large plate or flat work surface. Sprinkle with half of the cheese and half of the chiles. Cover with another tortilla and set aside. Repeat for the remaining 2 tortillas.

Carefully transfer the filled tortillas to the grill and cook, turning once, until they are nicely marked on both sides and the cheese is melted, about 2 minutes per side.

Cut each quesadilla into 6 to 8 wedges to serve as an appetizer; leave whole to serve as 2 individual portions. Serve with salsa.

Hatch *and* Mushroom Turnovers

makes 3 dozen appetizer servings

DOUGH

1½ (8-ounce) packages cream cheese, softened

2¼ cups all-purpose flour

6 ounces (1½ sticks) unsalted butter, softened

FILLING

2 tablespoons olive oil

1 cup chopped onion

1 pound mushrooms, chopped

3 Hatch Chiles, roasted, peeled, stemmed, seeded, and chopped
(see Hatch Chile Essentials, page 12)

¼ teaspoon salt

½ teaspoon Melissa's Hatch Chile Powder

2 tablespoons all-purpose flour

¼ cup sour cream

1 tablespoon unsalted butter, melted

Combine the cream cheese, flour, and butter in a bowl. Mix to form a dough, then shape into a ball, cover, and chill for 1 hour.

Preheat the oven to 400°F. Heat the olive oil in a large skillet over medium heat. Add the onions and sauté until golden. Stir in the mushrooms and sauté until softened, 3 minutes. Stir in the chiles, salt, and chile powder. Evenly sprinkle the mixture with the flour, then stir in the sour cream and remove the pan from the heat. Set aside.

On a lightly floured work surface, pat or roll the chilled dough out to a ⅛-inch thickness. Use a 3-inch biscuit cutter to cut the dough into 3 dozen circles. Spoon 1 teaspoon of the mushroom mixture on half of each dough circle. Fold the dough over the filling, pressing the edges together with a fork to seal.

Arrange the turnovers, spaced 1 inch apart, on ungreased baking sheets. Brush the tops of the turnovers with the melted butter. Bake for 15 to 20 minutes, or until the edges are lightly browned.

Layered Hatch Chile Spread

makes 16 appetizer servings

6 ounces (1½ sticks) unsalted butter, softened

2 (8-ounce) packages plus 6 ounces cream cheese, softened, divided

1 teaspoon salt, divided

¼ teaspoon pepper

1⅓ cups jarred sun-dried tomatoes in oil, drained

⅓ cup tomato paste

4 cloves garlic, chopped

5 Hatch Chiles, roasted, peeled, stemmed, and seeded
(see Hatch Chile Essentials, page 12)

¼ cup Melissa's Italian Pine Nuts

2 tablespoons olive oil

¼ cup grated Parmesan cheese

Cooking spray

Crackers or sliced baguette, for serving

In a mixing bowl, combine the butter with 2 cups of the cream cheese. Add ½ teaspoon of the salt and all of the pepper, then beat the mixture with an electric mixer at medium speed until creamy and thoroughly blended. Set aside.

Use a food processor to chop the sun-dried tomatoes. Add 6 tablespoons of the cream cheese, all of the tomato paste, and ¼ teaspoon of the salt to the food processor and process until the mixture is smooth, stopping to scrape down the sides of the bowl. Transfer the mixture to a clean bowl and set aside.

Wipe the bowl of the food processor clean, then process the garlic, chiles, pine nuts, olive oil, and Parmesan to a coarse purée. Add the remaining 6 tablespoons of cream cheese and the remaining ¼ teaspoon salt. Pulse just until blended, stopping to scrape down the sides.

Lightly coat a 6-inch springform pan with cooking spray. Spread ½ cup of the reserved butter mixture evenly across the bottom of the pan, then layer on half of the tomato mixture followed by another ½ cup of the butter mixture. Top with half of the chile mixture, then another ½ cup of the butter mixture. Layer on the remaining tomato mixture, another ½ cup of the butter mixture, then spread on the remaining chile mixture. Spread the last of the butter mixture over the top. Cover the layered dip with plastic wrap and refrigerate until chilled and firm, at least 8 hours.

To unmold the dip, run a knife gently around the edge of the pan to loosen the sides. Release and remove the springform, then carefully transfer the molded dip from the base of the pan to a serving tray. Serve with crackers or sliced baguette.

Hatch Chile Spinach Artichoke Dip

makes 2 cups

1 tablespoon olive oil

½ small onion, chopped

1 (6.5-ounce) jar marinated artichoke hearts, drained and chopped

1 (10-ounce) package frozen chopped spinach, thawed and drained

½ cup roasted, peeled, stemmed, seeded, and chopped Hatch Chiles
(see Hatch Chile Essentials, page 12)

¼ cup grated Parmesan cheese

2 cups shredded Jack cheese

½ cup whole milk

1 teaspoon Melissa's Hatch Chile Powder

Vegetables, tortilla chips, or crackers, for serving

In a large skillet, heat the oil over medium heat and sauté the onions until tender, about 5 minutes. Add the artichokes, spinach, and Hatch Chiles; cook, stirring frequently, just to heat through. Stir in the Parmesan, then add the Jack, milk, and Hatch Chile powder. Heat, stirring frequently, until the cheese is melted. Serve immediately with vegetables, tortilla chips, or crackers.

Hummus

makes 2 cups

2 cups drained canned garbanzo beans

⅓ cup tahini

¼ cup freshly squeezed lemon juice

1 teaspoon salt

2 cloves garlic, halved

1 tablespoon olive oil

Melissa's Hatch Chile Powder

Combine the garbanzo beans, tahini, lemon juice, salt, and garlic in food processor. Blend until smooth. Transfer the hummus to a serving bowl, drizzle with olive oil, and sprinkle with Hatch Chile powder.

Spicy Roasted Pepitas

makes 2 cups

2 cups fresh pumpkin seeds, rinsed and dried

2 tablespoons vegetable or olive oil

2 teaspoons Melissa's Hatch Chile Powder

1 teaspoon salt

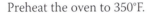

Preheat the oven to 350°F.

Put the pumpkin seeds in a medium bowl and drizzle with the oil. Add the salt and chile powder and toss to mix. Spread the pumpkin seeds on a large, rimmed baking sheet and roast for 8 minutes. Stir the seeds, then bake for 8 to 10 more minutes, or until they are lightly golden and crunchy.

Let the seeds cool completely before serving. Store in an airtight container.

Hatch Chile Cheese Ball

makes 1 cheese ball

4 Hatch Chiles, roasted, peeled, stemmed, seeded, and chopped *(see Hatch Chile Essentials, page 12)*

1½ pounds cheddar cheese, shredded

2 (8-ounce) packages cream cheese, softened

2 cloves garlic, minced

1 teaspoon salt

1 teaspoon Melissa's Hatch Chile Powder

2 cups Melissa's Italian Pine Nuts, lightly toasted and finely chopped *(see Note, page 98)*

Line a plate with wax paper.

In a large bowl, combine the chiles with the cheddar, cream cheese, garlic, salt, and chile powder. Mix well. Form the mixture into a ball and transfer to the paper-lined plate. Set the cheese ball in the freezer to chill until very cold, about 15 minutes.

Spread the chopped pine nuts on a large cutting board. Roll the chilled cheese ball in the pine nuts.

Serve with an assortment of crackers.

HATCH CHILE

SANDWICHES & WRAPS

Hatch Chile Bleu Cheese Sliders

Hatch Chile Bleu Cheese Sliders

makes 8 sliders

1 pound lean ground beef

1 cup crumbled Roquefort cheese

3 Hatch Chiles, roasted, peeled, stemmed, seeded, and chopped *(see Hatch Chile Essentials, page 12)*

Kosher salt and freshly ground pepper

8 sweet Hawaiian dinner rolls (such as King's brand), or other small dinner rolls, halved horizontally

Preheat a grill to high heat. Combine the beef, Roquefort, and chiles in a bowl. Mix well and shape into 8 small patties.

Grill the sliders to 160°F for medium, or to desired doneness. Serve on the dinner rolls with condiments as desired (i.e., ketchup, mustard, relish, tomato, onion, etc.).

Sloppy Joes

makes 4 sandwiches

1 pound lean ground beef

1 (10.75-ounce) can tomato soup

3 teaspoons prepared mustard

¼ teaspoon salt

1 pinch black pepper

2 tablespoons Melissa's Hatch Chile Powder

½ teaspoon garlic salt

4 hamburger buns, toasted

½ cup shredded cheddar cheese

Brown the ground beef in a nonstick skillet over medium-high heat, stirring to crumble, until it is cooked through. Drain off the rendered fat, then add the tomato soup, mustard, salt, pepper, Hatch Chile powder, and garlic salt. Simmer the meat mixture over low heat for 15 minutes. Serve on the toasted buns, topped with the cheese.

Hatch Chile Grilled Portobello Cheese "Burgers"

makes 4 sandwiches

4 Portobello mushrooms, stems and gills removed

2 tablespoons olive oil

2 tablespoons balsamic vinegar

Salt and freshly ground black pepper

4 slices Swiss cheese

1¼ cups mayonnaise

2 tablespoons fresh dill, chopped

2 cloves garlic, minced

4 hamburger buns

1 tomato, sliced crosswise into 4 rounds

4 Hatch Chiles, roasted, peeled, stemmed, and seeded
(see Hatch Chile Essentials, page 12)

Combine the mushrooms, olive oil, and vinegar in a large resealable plastic bag. Shake to mix, then set aside to marinate for 30 minutes.

Preheat a grill or broiler to medium-high. Season the mushrooms with salt and pepper. Grill the mushrooms, turning once, until they are nicely marked on both sides and fork-tender, about 5 minutes per side minutes. Remove the mushrooms from the grill and top each with a slice of cheese.

Whisk together the mayonnaise, dill, and garlic.

To assemble the "burgers," spread the buns with the mayonnaise and layer between each top and bottom bun a mushroom, a tomato slice, and a Hatch Chile.

Grilled Vegetable
and Hatch Chile Panini

makes 2 sandwiches

Extra-virgin olive oil

1 Portobello mushroom, stem and gills removed

1 onion, sliced

1 tomato, cut crosswise into thick slices

1 zucchini, cut lengthwise into thick slices

Melissa's My Grinder® Organic Garden Herb with Sea Salt

Melissa's My Grinder® Organic Rainbow Peppercorns

Mayonnaise, for spreading

4 thick slices rustic Italian bread

3 or 4 leaves red leaf lettuce

2 Hatch Chiles, roasted, peeled, stemmed, and seeded
(see Hatch Chile Essentials, page 12)

4 slices Muenster cheese

Preheat a grill to high heat. Brush the mushroom, onions, tomatoes, and zucchini with the olive oil and season with salt and pepper. Grill the vegetables until nicely marked on one side. Carefully flip them over and repeat. Transfer the grilled vegetables to a plate and let stand to drain off excess juices.

Spread mayonnaise on the 4 bread slices and top with each with a slice of Muenster. Layer half of the grilled vegetables onto 2 of the bread slices. Top each with lettuce and a Hatch Chile followed by the remaining bread slices.

Brush olive oil on the top and bottom of each sandwich. Set the sandwiches on the hot grill and weigh them down with a cast iron pan or other heatproof weight. When the cheese starts to melt and the bread is nicely marked, flip the sandwiches over, weigh them down, and grill them a few more minutes until they are well marked on the second side. Serve hot.

Note: *A sandwich press or other type of indoor grill is an easy alternative to the method described above.*

Hatch and Cheese Tacos

makes 12 tacos

2 teaspoons olive oil

1 large white onion, halved and cut into ¼-inch thick strips

12 Hatch Chiles, roasted, peeled, stemmed, seeded, and sliced lengthwise into ½-inch wide strips *(see Hatch Chile Essentials, page 12)*

½ teaspoon salt

¼ teaspoon black pepper

¾ cup heavy cream

12 corn tortillas

6 ounces queso fresco, crumbled

Heat the oil in a skillet over medium heat. Add the onions to the pan and sauté until they are translucent and begin to brown on the edges. Turn the heat down to low and add the chiles, salt, pepper, and cream to the pan. Cook the mixture over low heat just until the cream is heated through.

Wrap the corn tortillas in a clean, damp dishtowel and microwave on high for 1 minute; they should be steaming hot.

Fill each tortilla with equal amounts of the chile mixture. Sprinkle the queso fresco over the tortillas and serve immediately.

Ground Beef Tacos *with* Hatch Chiles

makes 12 tacos

1 pound lean ground beef

1 (1.25-ounce) package taco seasoning mix

12 taco shells, warmed

½ head iceberg lettuce, shredded

2 Roma tomatoes, diced

4 Hatch Chiles, roasted, peeled, stemmed, seeded, and chopped *(see Hatch Chile Essentials, page 12)*

1 small (2.25-ounce) can sliced black olives, drained

2 cups shredded cheddar cheese

Sour cream, for garnish

Quick Hatch Chile Salsa Fresca *(page 150)*

Brown the ground beef in a nonstick skillet over medium-high heat, stirring to crumble, until it is cooked through. Drain off the grease and stir in the taco seasoning. Fill the warm taco shells with the meat, lettuce, tomatoes, chiles, olives, and cheese. Top with sour cream and salsa.

Hatch Chile Chicken Burritos

makes 8 large burritos

2 tomatoes, chopped

½ cup roasted, peeled, stemmed, seeded, and chopped Hatch Chiles *(see Hatch Chile Essentials, page 12)*

⅓ cup sliced green onions

1 tablespoon chopped fresh cilantro *(optional)*

1 teaspoon olive oil

¾ pound boneless, skinless chicken breasts, cut into 1-inch cubes

2 tablespoons Melissa's Hatch Chile Powder

8 large (10-inch) flour tortillas

In a large bowl, combine the tomatoes, chiles, green onions, and cilantro. Set aside.

In a large skillet, heat the oil over medium-high heat. Add the chicken and cook about 2 minutes. Add 2 tablespoons of water and the Hatch Chile powder to the pan and continue cooking until the chicken is cooked through, about 7 minutes. Add the tomato mixture to the pan and stir to combine, then simmer the mixture for a few minutes to cook off the liquid.

Spoon about ½ cup filling onto each tortilla, fold in the top and bottom edges, and roll into burritos.

Shredded Beef Burritos
with Hatch Chiles

makes 6 burritos

1 pound boneless beef chuck steak

1 onion, halved

4 cloves garlic, halved

Salt and freshly ground
black pepper

6 large (10-inch) flour tortillas

2 fresh tomatoes, diced

½ head iceberg lettuce, shredded

4 Hatch Chiles, roasted, peeled,
stemmed, seeded, and chopped
(see Hatch Chile Essentials, page 12)

½ cup sour cream

1 cup shredded cheese, such as
Jack, cheddar, or a combination
of both

Place the beef in a large pot, season the meat all over with salt and pepper, then add enough cold water to cover it by 1 to 2 inches. Add the onion and garlic and bring the mixture to a boil, then reduce the heat to a simmer and cook for 1 hour.

Remove the pot from the heat. Drain the meat and let it cool. Remove and discard the onions and garlic. Use 2 forks to shred the beef.

Lay out the tortillas on a flat work surface. Divide the shredded beef among the 6 tortillas, piling the meat down the center of each tortilla.
Top each with tomatoes, lettuce, chiles, sour cream, and cheese. Roll up into burritos and enjoy.

Roasted Chile
and Cheddar Tamales

makes 12 tamales

1 Melissa's Authentic Tamale Kit

6 Hatch Chiles, roasted, peeled, stemmed and seeded *(see Hatch Chile Essentials, page 12)*

3 cups shredded cheddar cheese

Roasted Hatch and Tomatillo Salsa *(page 151)*, for serving

Prepare the corn masa according to the tamale kit package directions and spread over each cornhusk. Divide the roasted chiles and cheese among the 12 cornhusks, placing the filling down the center of each cornhusk. Fold and close the tamales carefully so they don't come open while steaming. Steam according to the tamale kit package instructions, for 45 minutes or until the masa is firm. Let the tamales sit 30 minutes before serving. Serve hot, with Roasted Hatch and Tomatillo Salsa.

Classic Grilled
Cheese Sandwich

makes 2 sandwiches

Unsalted butter, softened

4 slices sourdough bread

4 ounces cheddar cheese, cut into ⅓-inch thick slices

1 Hatch Chile, roasted, peeled, stemmed, seeded, and halved lengthwise *(see Hatch Chile Essentials, page 12)*

Set a large pan over medium-high heat and add enough butter to lightly coat the bottom of the pan. Layer the cheese and chiles onto 2 of the bread slices. Top with the remaining 2 slices of bread. Cook the sandwiches on one side, turning after 5 minutes or when the first side is golden brown and the cheese has begun to melt. Cook on the other side just until golden brown. Serve hot.

Black Bean *and* Hatch Chile Wraps

~~~~~~~~~~~~~ *makes 120 appetizer portions* ~~~~~~~~~~~~~

2 cups mayonnaise

2 tablespoons Dijon mustard

Freshly squeezed juice of
4 Key limes

4 cloves garlic, roasted and minced

3 tablespoons minced canned
chipotle chiles

1 (15-ounce) can black beans,
drained

½ (15.5-ounce) jar Melissa's
Fire Roasted Sweet Red Bell
Peppers, minced

4 Hatch Chiles, roasted, peeled,
stemmed, seeded, and chopped
(see Hatch Chile Essentials, page 12)

Salt and freshly ground
black pepper

1 head Napa cabbage, shredded

1 dozen large (10-inch)
flour tortillas

To make the aïoli, combine the mayonnaise, mustard, lime juice, garlic, and chipotles in a bowl and stir until well combined. Set aside in the refrigerator.

Combine the beans, roasted bell peppers, and Hatch Chiles in a bowl. Season to taste with salt and pepper.

Spread aïoli, then bean mixture on each tortilla. Top with Napa cabbage. Roll the tortillas up tightly, cut crosswise into 1-inch thick slices, and serve.

Note: *These wraps can also be served whole and are even better when garnished with a salsa or savory sauce.*

Chicken Lettuce Wraps

makes 4 to 6 servings

3 teaspoons cornstarch, divided

2 teaspoons plus 1 tablespoon cooking sherry, divided

Kosher salt and freshly ground black pepper

1½ pounds boneless skinless chicken breast, cut into ½-inch cubes

1 tablespoon hoisin sauce

1 tablespoon soy sauce

2 tablespoons oyster sauce

1 teaspoon granulated sugar

1 teaspoon sesame oil

4 tablespoons extra-virgin olive oil, divided

2 tablespoons unsalted butter, divided

1 teaspoon minced fresh ginger

4 cloves garlic, minced

2 fresh Hatch Chiles, roasted, peeled, stemmed, seeded, and, minced *(see Hatch Chile Essentials, page 12)*

1 Melissa's Perfect Sweet Onion, minced

10 button mushrooms, finely diced

1 (7.5-ounce) tub Melissa's Bamboo Shoots, drained

1 (7.5-ounce) tub Melissa's Waterchestnuts, drained

1 cup white rice, cooked and kept warm

10 large leaves romaine or other tender but sturdy lettuce, rinsed and dried

In a large resealable plastic bag, combine 1 teaspoon of the cornstarch and 2 teaspoons of the sherry with 2 teaspoons water. Seal the bag and gently squeeze to blend. Season the chicken with salt and pepper and add it to the bag. Seal the bag and set the chicken in the refrigerator to marinate for 30 minutes.

In a small bowl, whisk together the hoisin sauce, soy sauce, oyster sauce, sugar, sesame oil, the remaining tablespoon of sherry, and the remaining 2 teaspoons of cornstarch. Set aside.

In a wok, heat 2 tablespoons of the olive oil and 1 tablespoon of the butter. Add the marinated chicken and stir-fry over medium-high heat for 5 minutes, or until the chicken is fully cooked. Transfer the chicken to a bowl

continued

Chicken Lettuce Wraps continued

and set aside. Add the remaining 2 tablespoons of olive oil and the remaining tablespoon of butter to the wok and stir-fry the ginger, garlic, Hatch Chiles, onions, mushrooms, bamboo shoots, and waterchestnuts for 3 minutes.

Return the chicken to the wok. Pour all but a couple of tablespoons of the hoisin sauce mixture into the wok and cook until the mixture is heated through and the sauce is slightly thickened.

Stir the reserved sauce into the warm rice.

To serve, divide the chicken mixture and the rice among the lettuce leaves. Wrap the lettuce around the filling like a burrito.

Taco Sandwiches

makes 4 sandwiches

½ pound lean ground beef

1 tablespoon packaged taco seasoning mix

4 ounces cream cheese, softened

2 tablespoons Melissa's Sun Dried Tomato Pesto

4 small sandwich rolls

½ cup shredded iceberg lettuce

2 Hatch Chiles, roasted, peeled, and seeded *(see Hatch Chile Essentials, page 12)*

1 tomato, sliced

½ cup shredded cheese

Brown the ground beef in a nonstick skillet over medium-high heat, stirring to crumble, until it is cooked through. Drain off the grease, stir in the taco seasoning, and set aside to cool.

In a small bowl, mix together the cream cheese and pesto. Cut the rolls in half and spread with the pesto mixture.

Divide the ground beef among the bottom halves of the 4 rolls. Layer on the lettuce, chiles, tomato, and cheese, followed by the top halves of the rolls.

Grilled Sausage
and Veggie Sandwich

~~~~~~~~~~~~~~ *makes 4 sandwiches* ~~~~~~~~~~~~~~

¼ cup mayonnaise

3 cloves garlic, minced

Freshly squeezed juice of ½ lemon

4 spicy Italian sausages

Extra-virgin olive oil

1 zucchini, sliced lengthwise into ¼-inch thick slabs

1 yellow crookneck squash, sliced lengthwise into ¼-inch thick slabs

1 Melissa's Perfect Sweet Onion, sliced lengthwise into ¼-inch thick rounds

½ (5.5-ounce) jar Melissa's Fire Roasted Sweet Red Bell Peppers, drained

Salt and freshly ground black pepper

4 French bread rolls, split lengthwise

4 Hatch Chiles, roasted, peeled, stemmed, and seeded *(see Hatch Chile Essentials, page 12)*

4 slices Muenster cheese

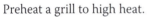

Preheat a grill to high heat.

Whisk together the mayonnaise, garlic, and lemon juice and set the mixture aside in the refrigerator.

Grill the sausages until they are completely cooked through. Set aside at room temperature while you grill the vegetables.

Brush the slices of zucchini, crookneck, and onion with olive oil and season with salt and pepper. Grill the vegetables on both sides, until heated through and nicely marked. Toss the grilled vegetables with the roasted red peppers.

To assemble the sandwiches, spread the mayonnaise on the rolls. Split each sausage lengthwise down the middle and set on a roll. Divide the grilled vegetables among the rolls, topping each with a Hatch Chile and a slice of Muenster.

Hatch Chile Taquitos

makes 4 servings

3 Hatch Chiles, roasted, peeled, stemmed, seeded, and chopped *(see Hatch Chile Essentials, page 12)*

1 cup Jack cheese

½ cup Tomatillo and Hatch Chile Verde Sauce *(page 152)*

1 small potato, diced and cooked

½ cup rehydrated Melissa's Roasted Sweet Corn *(see Note, page 36)*, or canned or thawed frozen corn

16 small corn tortillas

Oil, for frying

Mix the chiles, cheese, chile verde sauce, potatoes, and corn in a medium bowl. Spoon about 2 tablespoons of filling down the center of each tortilla and roll tightly, securing with a toothpick and placing seam-side down on a plate.

In a deep pot, heat ½ inch of oil to 350°F. Fry the taquitos 3 or 4 at a time until golden brown and crispy. Drain on paper towels and serve immediately.

Note: *Mix additional Tomatillo and Hatch Chile Verde Sauce with sour cream to make a dipping sauce for the taquitos.*

Roasted DYP Tamales
with Picante Cheese Sauce

makes 1 dozen tamales

2 pounds Melissa's Baby Dutch Yellow® Potatoes (DYPs), quartered

4 cloves garlic, peeled and left whole

2 tablespoons olive oil

Melissa's My Grinder® Organic Garlic & Herbs with Sea Salt

Melissa's My Grinder® Organic Rainbow Peppercorns

1 small bunch fresh rosemary, stemmed and finely chopped

1 Melissa's Authentic Tamale Kit

1 pound VELVEETA®, cubed

½ cup whole milk

2 Hatch Chiles, roasted, peeled, stemmed, seeded, and chopped *(see Hatch Chile Essentials, page 12)*

1 pinch Melissa's Hatch Chile Powder

Preheat the oven to 400°F.

Arrange the potatoes cut-side up on a large baking sheet. Add the garlic cloves, drizzle on the olive oil and season the mixture with the herb salt and pepper. Roast the potatoes until they are golden brown and soft, 10 to 13 minutes.

Combine the hot potatoes in a bowl with the rosemary and toss to mix. Taste and adjust seasonings with additional salt and pepper.

Assemble the tamales as directed on the tamale kit package, using the potato mixture for filling. Then wrap the husks and steam as directed on the package, for about 45 minutes or until the masa is firm.

To make the sauce, combine the VELVEETA® and the milk in a medium saucepan over medium-low heat and cook, stirring frequently, until most of the cheese is melted. Stir in the Hatch Chiles and heat until the cheese is completely melted, then add the chile powder and mix well.

Drizzle the hot cheese sauce over the tamales and serve immediately.

Hatch Steak Sandwich

makes 4 sandwiches

½ teaspoon salt

½ teaspoon black pepper

1 teaspoon Melissa's Hatch Chile Powder

½ teaspoon onion powder

½ teaspoon garlic powder

½ teaspoon dried thyme

1 pound beef sirloin, thinly sliced into 2-inch long strips

3 tablespoons vegetable oil, divided

1 onion, sliced

2 Hatch Chiles, roasted, peeled, stemmed, seeded, and halved *(see Hatch Chile Essentials, page 12)*

4 thin slices Swiss cheese

4 hoagie rolls, split lengthwise

In a large bowl, mix together the salt, pepper, Hatch Chile powder, onion powder, garlic powder, and thyme. Add the beef strips and toss to coat. Sprinkle the seasoning mixture over the meat. In a skillet over medium-high heat, heat 1½ tablespoons of the oil until shimmering. Add the beef, sauté it to desired doneness, and remove it from the pan and set aside.

Add the remaining 1½ tablespoons of oil to the skillet, and sauté the onions and Hatch Chiles until the unions are softened, about 5 minutes.

Preheat the oven to broil.

Divide the meat among the bottoms of the 4 rolls, layer on the onions and Hatch Chiles, then top with sliced cheese. Set on a baking sheet and broil to melt the cheese. Cover with tops of rolls and serve.

HATCH CHILE

SALADS

Hatch Lentil and Edamame Salad

Hatch Lentil
and Edamame Salad

makes 8 servings

1 (17.63-ounce) package Melissa's Steamed Ready-to-Eat Lentils

1 (10-ounce) package Melissa's Shelled Edamame

1 cup sliced roasted red bell peppers

½ cup roasted, peeled, stemmed, seeded, and chopped Hatch Chiles *(see Hatch Chile Essentials, page 12)*

½ cup rice vinegar

¼ cup olive oil

Salt and freshly ground black pepper

In a large bowl, gently stir together the lentils, edamame, red bell peppers, and Hatch Chiles. In a separate bowl, whisk together the vinegar and oil. Pour the dressing over the salad, mix together gently, and season to taste with salt and pepper. Refrigerate until ready to serve.

Spicy Cashew Quinoa

makes 4 to 6 servings

1 (8-ounce) package Melissa's Quinoa with Garlic & Herb Seasoning Packet

1 cup red Melissa's Muscato Grapes, halved

1 fresh Hatch Chile, minced *(see Hatch Chile Essentials, page 12)*

¼ cup cashews, chopped

⅓ cup crumbled Feta cheese

Prepare the quinoa according to the package instructions; let cool to room temperature.

In a medium bowl, combine the quinoa with the grapes, chiles, cashews, and Feta. Gently mix to combine.

Note: *If you want to add zip to this dish, sprinkle it with a little freshly squeezed lemon juice.*

Hatch Chile *and* Hominy Salad

makes 8 servings

SALAD

1 (10-ounce) package Melissa's Shelled Edamame

2 (15-ounce) cans yellow hominy, rinsed and drained

3 small bell peppers (a combination of red, yellow, and orange), diced

1 small red onion, diced

3 Hatch Chiles, roasted, peeled, stemmed, seeded, and chopped *(see Hatch Chile Essentials, page 12)*

¼ cup chopped fresh cilantro

DRESSING

½ cup rice wine vinegar

¼ cup freshly squeezed lime juice

¼ cup vegetable oil

2 teaspoons Melissa's Hatch Chile Powder

½ teaspoon ground cumin

Mix the edamame, hominy, bell peppers, onion, chiles, and cilantro together in a bowl. In a separate bowl, whisk together the vinegar, lime juice, oil, chile powder, and cumin. Pour the dressing over the salad. Chill at least 4 hours before serving.

Note: *Add cooked shrimp to make this a main dish.*

Hatch Chile Summer Salad

makes 8 servings

SALAD

3 cups cooked rice, cooled

2 cups fresh corn kernels, cooked and cooled

½ cup roasted, peeled, stemmed, seeded, and chopped Hatch Chiles
(see Hatch Chile Essentials, page 12)

½ cup drained, chopped Melissa's Pimientos del Piquillo

⅓ cup chopped red bell pepper

⅓ cup sliced green onions

2 small tomatoes, chopped

1 teaspoon Melissa's Hatch Chile Powder

8 ounces queso fresco or mild Feta cheese, crumbled

DRESSING

3 tablespoons lime juice

3 tablespoons olive oil

1 teaspoon crushed garlic

Combine the rice, corn, Hatch Chiles, piquillo peppers, bell pepper, onions, tomatoes, and Hatch Chile powder in a large bowl. In a separate bowl, whisk together the lime juice, oil, and garlic. Pour the dressing over the salad and mix well. Just before serving, add the cheese and toss lightly to combine.

Green Chile
and Tomato Salad

makes 6 servings

1¼ cup vegetable oil

2 tablespoons freshly squeezed lemon juice

1 tablespoon chopped fresh oregano

1 pinch plus ¼ teaspoon kosher salt

¼ teaspoon black pepper

2 tablespoons cider vinegar or white wine vinegar

1 tablespoon cilantro leaves, chopped

6 large tomatoes, each cut crosswise into 8 slices

2 Hatch Chiles, roasted, peeled, stemmed, seeded, and diced *(see Hatch Chile Essentials, page 12)*

1 yellow bell pepper, diced

1 cucumber, diced

½ small onion, diced

To prepare the dressing, whisk together the oil, lemon juice, oregano, pinch of salt, black pepper, vinegar, and cilantro.

Combine the tomatoes, chiles, bell peppers, cucumbers, and onions in a salad bowl, season with the remaining ¼ teaspoon of salt. Drizzle the dressing over the salad and toss gently to coat.

Twice-Fried DYP Salad

makes 4 to 6 servings

1 quart vegetable oil, for frying

1½ pounds Melissa's Baby Dutch Yellow® Potatoes (DYPs), halved

Kosher salt

1 Melissa's Perfect Sweet Onion, diced

1 cup mayonnaise

8 slices smoked bacon, cooked crispy, drained, and chopped

¾ cup sweet pickle relish

3 Hatch Chiles, roasted, peeled, stemmed, seeded, and chopped
(see Hatch Chile Essentials, page 12)

Freshly ground black pepper

Preheat the oil to 350°F in a fryer or deep pot.

Fry the potatoes, in batches if necessary, until golden brown and fork-tender. Drain them on a paper towel-lined plate to absorb excess oil.

Using a kitchen mallet, smash the fried potatoes, one by one. Then carefully refry them until they are crispy and golden brown. Drain on fresh paper towels and immediately season them with salt. Once the potatoes are cool, transfer them to a bowl. Add the onions, mayonnaise, bacon, pickles, and chiles. Mix gently. Season to taste with pepper and additional salt.

Note: *If you don't have a kitchen mallet, the bottom of a frying pan works just fine for smashing the potatoes.*

Baby Heirloom Tomato *and* Grilled Corn Salad

makes 8 servings

4 ears corn, husks and silk removed

2 (1-pound packages) Melissa's Baby Heirloom Tomatoes, halved

3 cloves garlic, minced

2 Hatch Chiles, roasted, peeled, stemmed, seeded, and diced *(see Hatch Chile Essentials, page 12)*

½ cup fresh basil leaves, cut into ribbons *(see Note below)*

2 tablespoons olive oil

4 tablespoons seasoned rice vinegar

Salt and black pepper

Preheat a grill to high.

Grill the corn until lightly charred. Let cool. Cut the kernels from the cobs.

In a large bowl, combine the corn kernels with the tomatoes. Add the garlic, chiles, basil, oil, and vinegar. Toss, seasoning to taste with salt and pepper, and serve.

Note: *To cut the basil into ribbons, stack the leaves on top of one other, roll them up tightly, and slice crosswise with a very sharp knife.*

Edamame
and Fresh Hatch Salad

~~~~~~~~~~~~~~ *makes 6 to 8 servings* ~~~~~~~~~~~~~~

1 (14.75-ounce) jar marinated artichoke hearts, drained

½ cup freshly squeezed lemon juice

½ cup freshly squeezed lime juice

Salt and freshly ground black pepper

1 tablespoon granulated sugar, plus more as desired

½ cup extra-virgin olive oil

¼ cup minced shallots

1 (10-ounce) package Melissa's Shelled Edamame

4 fresh Hatch Chiles, stemmed, seeded, and thinly sliced
(see Hatch Chile Essentials, page 12)

~~~~~~

Preheat the oven to 425°F. Spread the artichokes hearts in a single layer on a baking sheet and roast 8 to 10 minutes.

In a small bowl, whisk together the lemon and lime juice, salt, pepper, sugar, olive oil, and shallots. If the dressing is too tart, add more sugar to taste. In another bowl, toss together the artichoke hearts, edamame, and chiles. Pour the dressing over the salad, toss gently, and adjust the seasonings to taste. Refrigerate until well chilled. Serve cold.

Nopalitos Salad

makes 6 servings

2 cups trimmed, chopped nopales (cactus paddles)

Salt

1 small onion, chopped

2 fresh Roma tomatoes, cubed

1 tablespoon fresh chopped cilantro

2 Hatch Chiles, roasted, peeled, stemmed, seeded, and chopped *(see Hatch Chile Essentials, page 12)*

1 avocado, cubed

Freshly squeezed juice of 1 lime

Salt

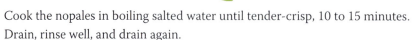

Cook the nopales in boiling salted water until tender-crisp, 10 to 15 minutes. Drain, rinse well, and drain again.

Combine the nopalitos, onions, tomatoes, cilantro, chiles, avocado, and lime juice in a salad bowl. Toss together, seasoning to taste with salt. Refrigerate until well chilled. Serve cold.

Melissa's Six Bean Salad

makes 4 to 6 servings

1 (12.3-ounce) package
Melissa's Steamed Ready-to-Eat
Six Bean Medley

2 fresh Hatch Chiles, chopped
(see Hatch Chile Essentials, page 12)

½ red bell pepper, chopped

2 green onions, chopped

1 stalk celery, chopped

½ Roma tomato, seeded
and chopped

1 serrano chile, chopped

2 tablespoons olive oil

1 tablespoon balsamic vinegar

Kosher salt and freshly ground
black pepper

In a large bowl, combine the beans, Hatch Chiles, bell peppers, onions, celery, tomatoes, and serranos. Toss gently. In a separate bowl, whisk together the olive oil and balsamic vinegar. Pour the dressing over the salad and gently toss to combine, seasoning to taste with salt and pepper before serving.

SIDES

Sautéed Green Beans *and* **Peppers**

makes 4 servings

2 tablespoons extra-virgin olive oil

2 tablespoons unsalted butter

1 pound fresh green beans, trimmed

1 pound Melissa's Veggie Sweet Mini Peppers, cut into thin rings

1 fresh Hatch Chile, cut into thin rings *(see Hatch Chile Essentials, page 12)*

Freshly squeezed juice of 1 lemon

1 (3-ounce) package Melissa's Pine Nuts, toasted *(see Note, page 98)*

Melissa's My Grinder® Organic Garlic & Herbs with Sea Salt

Melissa's My Grinder® Organic Rainbow Peppercorns

In a large sauté pan, heat the oil and butter over medium heat until the butter is melted. Add the beans and cook until tender-crisp. Add the peppers, chiles, lemon juice, and pine nuts to the pan. Cook the mixture, stirring often, just until it is heated through and beans are tender-crisp. Season to taste with the herb salt and pepper and serve hot.

Note: *For a spicier finish, sprinkle with Hatch Chile powder.*

Hatch Chile *and* Potato Gratin

makes 6 servings

Unsalted butter

4 large russet potatoes, peeled and thinly sliced

1½ cups grated cheddar cheese

2 Hatch Chiles, roasted, peeled, stemmed, seeded, and chopped
(see Hatch Chile Essentials, page 12)

Salt and freshly ground black pepper

1 cup chicken broth

1 cup heavy cream

Preheat the oven to 400°F.

Butter an 11 by 7-inch baking dish. Layer in a third of the potatoes, then half of the cheese, followed by half of the chiles. Season with salt and pepper. Layer in another third of the potatoes, then the remaining cheese and chiles. Top with the remaining potato slices.

In a separate bowl, whisk together the broth and cream, then pour it over the potato mixture.

Bake the gratin 45 minutes, or until the potatoes are tender, the liquid is absorbed, and the top has browned. Let stand for 5 minutes before serving.

Roasted DYPs, Turnips *and* Butternut Squash

makes 8 servings

1 pound Melissa's Baby Dutch Yellow® Potatoes (DYPs), cut in quarters

1½ cups peeled, chopped turnips

1½ cups peeled, chopped butternut squash

1½ cups peeled, chopped South African Baby Pineapple or golden pineapple

2 tablespoons extra-virgin olive oil

1 pinch sea salt

2 teaspoons freshly ground black pepper

2 teaspoons Melissa's Hatch Chile Powder

2 Hatch Chiles, roasted, peeled, stemmed, seeded, and chopped *(see Hatch Chile Essentials, page 12)*

Freshly grated zest of 1 lime

6 fresh basil leaves, cut into ribbons *(see Note, page 78)*

Preheat the oven to 425°F. In a large bowl, combine the potatoes, turnips, squash, pineapple, olive oil, salt, pepper, and chile powder. Spread the mixture in a single layer on baking sheets. Roast for about 15 minutes, or until the vegetables are fork-tender.

Transfer the potato mixture to a serving bowl. Stir in the chiles and lime zest. Garnish with the basil and serve.

Note: *This dish is a tasty combination of savory and sweet.*

Fresh Hatch Roasted Melissa's Baby Dutch Yellow® Potatoes

makes 6 servings

2 pounds Melissa's Baby Dutch Yellow® Potatoes, halved

4 fresh Hatch Chiles, stemmed, seeded, and sliced into rings
(see Hatch Chile Essentials, page 12)

¼ cup extra-virgin olive oil

Kosher salt and freshly ground black pepper

Preheat the oven to 425°F. Combine the potatoes, chiles, and olive oil in a mixing bowl. Season with salt and pepper and stir to coat. Spread the potatoes in a single even layer on a baking sheet. Roast the potatoes until fork-tender and golden brown, 15 to 20 minutes. Serve hot.

Calabacitas

makes 4 to 6 servings

2 tablespoons olive oil

1 onion, chopped

2 cloves garlic, minced

4 Hatch Chiles, roasted, peeled, stemmed, seeded, and chopped
(see Hatch Chile Essentials, page 12)

2 pounds Tatuma squash, chopped

¼ teaspoon black pepper

¼ teaspoon dried oregano

½ teaspoon salt

1 (14-ounce) can diced tomatoes, with juice

½ cup shredded cheddar cheese

Heat the oil in large saucepan over medium heat. Add the onion and sauté onion until softened, about 5 minutes. Add the garlic and sauté 1 minute more, being careful not to let the garlic brown. Add the chiles and the squash and sauté 5 minutes more. Stir in the black pepper, oregano, salt, and tomatoes. Bring the mixture to a boil, then lower the heat and simmer 15 minutes, or until the squash is tender. Remove the pan from the heat, stir in the cheese, and serve.

Note: *Tatuma squash is also known as Mexican zucchini or white zucchini. Green zucchini can be substituted, but Tatuma has a milder, sweeter flavor.*

Hatch *and* Celery Root Mash

makes 4 servings

2 celery roots, peeled and cubed

2 Yukon gold potatoes, peeled and cubed

2 teaspoons kosher salt

1 cup whole milk

4 tablespoons (½ stick) unsalted butter

½ cup roasted, peeled, stemmed, seeded, and chopped Hatch Chiles
(see Hatch Chile Essentials, page 12)

Melissa's My Grinder® Organic Garlic & Herbs with Sea Salt

Melissa's My Grinder® Organic Rainbow Peppercorns

Combine the celery root and the potatoes in a pot and cover them with cold water. Add the salt, bring the water to a medium boil, and cook until the vegetables are fork-tender, about 10 minutes. Drain the vegetables, transfer them to a serving bowl, and mash with a potato masher or a fork.

In a saucepan, combine the milk and butter and heat over medium heat until steaming hot but not boiling.

Gradually add just enough of the hot milk and butter mixture to the mash, stirring constantly, to achieve desired consistency. Serve hot.

Note: *For a lighter version use chicken or vegetable broth in place of the milk and butter.*

Hatch Chile Polenta Hash

makes 6 servings

3 tablespoons extra-virgin olive oil, plus more as needed

2 tablespoons unsalted butter

1 (1-pound) package Melissa's Organic Sun-Dried Tomato Polenta, cubed

1 Melissa's Perfect Sweet Onion, minced

2 Hatch Chiles, roasted, peeled, stemmed, seeded, and chopped *(see Hatch Chile Essentials, page 12)*

2 teaspoons Melissa's Hatch Chile Powder

1 clove garlic, minced

2 cups cherry tomatoes, halved

1 (15-ounce) can black beans, drained

In a large sauté pan over medium-high heat, combine the oil and butter. When the butter is melted, swirl to blend with the oil and continue to heat until shimmering, then add the polenta. Cook the polenta, carefully stirring to prevent sticking, until it is golden brown and slightly crisp. Remove the polenta from the pan and set it aside.

Add more oil if the pan is becoming dry, then add the onions, chiles, and chile powder. Sauté the mixture until the onions are tender, about 5 minutes. Stir in the garlic and cook for an additional 2 minutes, stirring constantly to keep the garlic from browning. Add the tomatoes, beans, and polenta and stir gently to combine. Cook until everything is heated through. Serve hot.

Marco's Baby Dutch Yellow® Potatoes *with* Roasted Hatch Chile Vinaigrette

makes 10 to 12 servings

SALAD

3 pounds Melissa's Baby Dutch Yellow® Potatoes, halved

2 cloves garlic, chopped

5 tablespoons extra-virgin olive oil, divided

Salt and freshly ground black pepper

1 Melissa's Perfect Sweet Onion, julienned

1 pound roasted, peeled, stemmed, and seeded and chopped Hatch Chiles *(see Hatch Chile Essentials, page 13)*

VINAIGRETTE

2 cups seasoned rice vinegar

½ cup granulated sugar

½ pound roasted, peeled, stemmed, seeded, and minced Hatch Chiles *(see Hatch Chile Essentials, page 12)*

2 cloves garlic, chopped

1¾ cups vegetable oil

Salt and freshly ground black pepper

Preheat the oven to 350°F. In a large bowl, toss together the potatoes, garlic, and 3 tablespoons of the olive oil. Spread the potatoes in a single layer on large baking sheets and season generously with salt and pepper. Roast the potatoes for 25 minutes, or until they are fork-tender. Let cool.

To caramelize the onions, sauté them for about 15 minutes in the remaining 2 tablespoons of olive oil over medium heat, stirring only occasionally. The onions will begin to soften, then start to turn a little brown. As the onions darken, continue cooking

continued

for about 10 more minutes, stirring more frequently to prevent them from burning. When caramelized, the onions will be deeply browned and intensely flavorful. Remove the pan from the heat and stir in the chopped Hatch Chiles.

To make the vinaigrette, whisk together the vinegar, sugar, minced Hatch Chiles, and garlic in a medium bowl. Slowly drizzle in the oil, whisking constantly to emulsify. Season with salt and pepper to taste.

To assemble the salad, gently toss together the potatoes and the onion and chile mixture. Pour the vinaigrette over the salad, give it a gentle toss to coat, and serve warm or at room temperature.

Rajas

makes 4 to 6 servings

2 teaspoons olive oil

1 large white onion, cut into ¼-inch slices

12 Hatch Chiles, roasted, peeled, stemmed, seeded, and cut into long, ¼-inch-wide strips *(see Hatch Chile Essentials, page 12)*

⅓ cup heavy cream or half-and-half

½ teaspoon salt

¼ teaspoon black pepper

Heat a large skillet over medium heat and drizzle in the oil. When the oil begins to shimmer, add the onions to the pan and cook them until they are translucent and beginning to brown at the edges, 3 to 5 minutes. Turn the heat down to low and add the chiles to the pan. Then stir in the cream and season the mixture with the salt and pepper. Cook the rajas over low heat until the cream is heated through, 2 to 3 minutes.

Note: *This side dish is perfect with steak or as a filling for tacos.*

Hatch Chile Rice

makes 6 servings

2 cups chicken broth

2 Hatch Chiles, roasted, peeled, stemmed, and seeded *(see Hatch Chile Essentials, page 12)*

1 small onion, diced

1 cup uncooked white rice

½ teaspoon salt

½ teaspoon ground cumin

3 green onions, sliced

In a blender, combine the broth, chiles, and onions and purée until blended.

In a large saucepan, combine the chile purée with the rice, salt, and cumin. Bring the mixture to a boil, then turn the heat down to low, cover, and simmer until the liquid is absorbed and the rice is tender, about 18 to 20 minutes. Garnish with the green onions.

Hatch Chile Mexican Rice

makes 4 servings

1 tablespoon olive oil

1 cup diced onion

½ cup diced carrot

2 cloves garlic, minced

1 cup uncooked long-grain rice

¾ cup diced fresh tomatoes

1 teaspoon salt

2 Hatch Chiles, roasted, peeled, stemmed, seeded, and chopped *(see Hatch Chile Essentials, page 12)*

2 cups vegetable broth

1 teaspoon chopped fresh oregano

Heat the olive oil in a large saucepan over medium-high heat. Add the onions, carrots, and garlic; sauté 8 minutes, or until the onion is soft and translucent. Stir in the rice, tomatoes, salt, chiles, and vegetable broth. Bring the mixture to a boil, reduce the heat to low, cover, and simmer 18 to 20 minutes, or until the rice is tender and most of the liquid is absorbed. Stir in the oregano and serve hot.

Hatch Chile *and* DYPs

makes 6 servings

2 pounds Melissa's Baby Dutch Yellow® Potatoes (DYPs)

1 tablespoon salt, plus to taste

1 cup roasted, peeled, stemmed, seeded, and chopped Hatch Chiles
(see Hatch Chile Essentials, page 12)

3 small tomatoes, chopped

2 cloves garlic, minced

2½ cups vegetable broth

In a large saucepan, combine the potatoes with the salt and enough cold water to cover by 1 inch. Bring to a boil and cook until tender, about 10 minutes. Drain and let cool, then halve the potatoes and return them to the pan. Add the tomatoes, garlic, and vegetable broth to the pan. Cook over medium heat about 15 minutes, stirring frequently, until the potatoes are soft and the sauce has thickened. Season to taste with additional salt before serving.

Hatch Chile Texas Beans

makes 8 servings

1 pound dried pinto beans

2 quarts water

2 cups canned whole tomatoes, chopped

1 (8-ounce) can tomato sauce

4 Hatch Chiles, roasted, peeled, stemmed, seeded, and chopped *(see Hatch Chile Essentials, page 12)*

1 large onion, chopped

2 cloves garlic, minced

1 teaspoon salt

1 teaspoon ground cumin

1 teaspoon Melissa's Hatch Chile Powder

Cooked rice, for serving

Combine the beans and water in a large pot or Dutch oven and bring to a boil over high heat. Reduce the heat, cover, and simmer the beans for 2 hours, or until they are tender.

Stir in the tomatoes and their juice, tomato sauce, onions, garlic, salt, cumin, and chile powder. Return the beans to a simmer and continue cooking, uncovered, stirring often, for another 90 minutes, or until mixture is thickened. Serve over rice.

Southwestern-Style Black Beans

makes 4 servings

2 tablespoons extra-virgin olive oil

½ Melissa's Perfect Sweet Onion, finely diced

2 cloves garlic, minced

2 Hatch Chiles, roasted, peeled, stemmed, seeded, and chopped *(see Hatch Chile Essentials, page 12)*

Kosher salt and black pepper

1 (14.5-ounce) can vegetable broth

1 (15-ounce) can black beans, drained

1 (15-ounce) can cannellini beans, drained

1 chipotle chile in adobo, minced

1 tablespoon Melissa's Hatch Chile Powder

2 teaspoon dried oregano

1 teaspoon ground coriander

1 teaspoon ground cumin

Heat the olive oil in a large skillet over medium-high heat. Add the onions, garlic, and Hatch Chiles to the pan, season with salt and pepper, and sauté for 2 minutes. Add the broth, beans, chipotles, chile powder, and spices to the pan. Bring the mixture to a boil, simmer for 15 minutes, and serve.

Hatch Chile Mashed Potatoes

makes 4 to 6 servings

3 pounds Yukon gold potatoes, peeled

4 tablespoons (½ stick) unsalted butter

1 cup whole milk, warmed

1 cup shredded sharp cheddar cheese

4 Hatch Chiles, roasted, peeled, stemmed, seeded, and chopped
(see Hatch Chile Essentials, page 12)

½ teaspoon ground cumin

Kosher salt and freshly ground black pepper

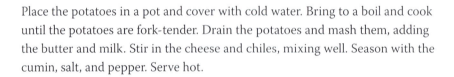

Place the potatoes in a pot and cover with cold water. Bring to a boil and cook until the potatoes are fork-tender. Drain the potatoes and mash them, adding the butter and milk. Stir in the cheese and chiles, mixing well. Season with the cumin, salt, and pepper. Serve hot.

Twice-Baked Potatoes

makes 4 servings

4 large baking potatoes

3 ounces cream cheese, softened

2 Hatch Chiles, roasted, peeled, stemmed, seeded, and chopped
(see Hatch Chile Essentials, page 12)

3 tablespoons unsalted butter

2 tablespoons sour cream

½ teaspoon salt

1 pinch black pepper

Melissa's Hatch Chile Powder

Preheat the oven to 400°F.

Pierce the skin of each potato a few times with a fork. Bake the potatoes 1 hour, or until fork-tender. Let cool slightly.

Turn the oven down to 375°F.

Split the potatoes lengthwise. Scoop out the insides and transfer to a mixing bowl, reserving the skins. Add the cream cheese, chiles, butter, sour cream, salt, and pepper. Beat well with an electric mixer. Scoop the potato mixture into the reserved skins. Sprinkle with Hatch Chile powder and bake until lightly browned, 5 to 7 minutes.

Hatch Chile Pesto Pasta

makes 6 servings

8 Hatch Chiles, roasted, peeled, stemmed, and seeded *(see Hatch Chile Essentials, page 12)*

½ cup Melissa's Pine Nuts, toasted *(see Note below)*

6 cloves roasted garlic

¼ cup grated Parmesan cheese, plus more as desired

¼ cup olive oil

Salt and freshly ground black pepper

1 pound spaghetti, cooked and drained

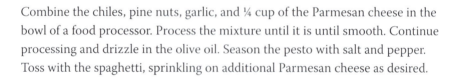

Combine the chiles, pine nuts, garlic, and ¼ cup of the Parmesan cheese in the bowl of a food processor. Process the mixture until it is until smooth. Continue processing and drizzle in the olive oil. Season the pesto with salt and pepper. Toss with the spaghetti, sprinkling on additional Parmesan cheese as desired.

Note: *Toasting pine nuts enhances their flavor. It is easiest to do this in a dry skillet over medium-low heat. Shake the skillet frequently to ensure even browning—the pine nuts are small and full of rich oil, and they will burn quickly if you don't watch carefully. When the nuts are fragrant and lightly browned, take the pan off the heat. Cool and use immediately.*

Stuffed Zucchini

makes 12 servings

Vegetable oil

6 zucchinis

Olive oil, for sautéing

1 red bell pepper, chopped

1 Melissa's Perfect Sweet Onion, chopped

3 large cloves garlic, chopped

½ pound mushrooms, chopped

3 Hatch Chiles, roasted, peeled, stemmed, seeded, and chopped
(see Hatch Chile Essentials, page 12)

2 medium tomatoes, or 4 to 6 plum tomatoes, chopped

Salt and freshly ground black pepper

½ cup breadcrumbs

Preheat the oven to 350°F. Lightly oil a large roasting pan or baking sheet.

Cut the zucchini in half lengthwise. Using a paring knife, carefully hollow out the zucchini, leaving the sides and bottom about ¼-inch thick. Chop and reserve the scooped-out zucchini flesh. Arrange the zucchini shells on the prepared pan.

Heat the olive oil in large sauté pan over medium-high heat. Stir in the bell peppers and onions. Cook until the onions are soft, 5 to 7 minutes. Add the garlic, mushrooms, chiles, and reserved zucchini flesh to the pan and cook the mixture until the mushrooms are tender. Add the tomatoes and season to taste with salt and pepper. Simmer uncovered for about 15 minutes. Adjust seasoning to taste. If there is a lot of liquid, drain off the excess through a colander. Mix in the breadcrumbs.

Fill the zucchini shells with the vegetable mixture. Bake for 30 to 45 minutes, until the shells are tender but still holding their shape.

Hatch Mac 'n Cheese

makes 8 servings

1 tablespoon vegetable oil

4 Hatch Chiles, roasted, peeled, stemmed, seeded, and chopped *(see Hatch Chile Essentials, page 12)*

2 cups canned tomato sauce

1 pound elbow macaroni, cooked according to package directions

1 cup shredded cheddar cheese

Salt and freshly ground black pepper

Heat the oil in large saucepan over medium heat. Add the Hatch Chile to the pan and sauté for 3 minutes. Add the tomato sauce and bring the mixture to a boil. Add the macaroni and cook, stirring constantly, until the mixture is heated through. Remove the pan from the heat and stir in the cheese. Season to taste with salt and pepper and serve hot.

Classic Mac 'n Cheese *with* Hatch

makes 6 to 8 servings

3 tablespoons unsalted butter or margarine

¼ cup finely chopped onion

2 tablespoons all-purpose flour

½ teaspoon salt

⅛ teaspoon pepper

2 cups whole milk

2 cups shredded mild cheddar cheese, divided

2 cups elbow macaroni, cooked and drained

4 Hatch Chiles, roasted, peeled, stemmed, seeded, and chopped *(see Hatch Chile Essentials, page 12)*

Preheat the oven to 350°F.

Melt the butter in a medium saucepan over medium heat. Cook the onion in the melted butter for 5 minutes, or until tender. Stir in the flour, salt, and pepper. Gradually add the milk and cook, stirring occasionally, until thickened, 7 to 10 minutes.

Remove the milk mixture from the heat. Add 1½ cups of the cheese and stir until the cheese is melted.

Combine the cheese sauce with the cooked macaroni and chiles. Mix well. Transfer the macaroni to a 1½-quart casserole and top with the remaining cheese. Bake 30 minutes or until the cheese is bubbly and lightly browned.

Spaghetti *with* Spicy Tomato Sauce

makes 4 servings

1 tablespoon unsalted butter

1 tablespoon extra-virgin olive oil

1 Melissa's Perfect Sweet Onion, finely diced

2 cloves garlic, minced

3 Hatch Chiles, roasted, peeled, stemmed, seeded, and chopped *(see Hatch Chile Essentials, page 12)*

1 8-ounce package button mushrooms, trimmed and left whole

¼ cup sherry

1 (14.5-ounce) can diced tomatoes

½ pound uncooked spaghetti

6 fresh basil leaves, cut into ribbons *(see Note, page 78)*

Salt and freshly ground black pepper

Put a large pot of water on to boil.

Combine the butter and olive oil in a sauté pan and heat over medium heat until the butter is melted. Add the onion and cook until translucent, about 5 minutes. Add the garlic, chiles, and mushrooms and cook until the mushrooms are softened. Add the sherry and sauté until most of the liquid has evaporated. Stir in the tomatoes and simmer the mixture for 15 minutes.

While the sauce cooks, prepare the spaghetti according to the package directions.

Season the sauce to taste with salt and pepper and stir in the basil. Toss the sauce with the spaghetti and serve.

Mexican Corn on the Cob

makes 6 servings

6 ears corn, unhusked

4 tablespoons (½ stick) unsalted
butter, softened

6 tablespoons mayonnaise, divided

½ cup crumbled Cotija cheese
or shredded Parmesan cheese

Melissa's Hatch Chile Powder

1 lime wedge

Preheat the oven to 350°F.

Roast the corn for 25 minutes. Let cool for 5 minutes, then pull the husks down in layers, leaving them attached to the base of the cob. Remove the silk and discard. While the corn is still warm, spread each ear with some of the butter and 1 tablespoon of the mayonnaise. Sprinkle each ear of corn with cheese, then dust with a little Hatch Chile powder. Finish with a squirt of lime.

ENTREES

HATCH CHILE

Hatch *and* Mushroom– Stuffed Pork Tenderloin

makes about 6 servings

2 tablespoons unsalted butter

2 packages dried oyster mushrooms, reconstituted *(see Note below)*

2 cloves garlic, minced

1 tablespoon dry sherry

Melissa's My Grinder® Organic Garlic & Herbs with Sea Salt

Melissa's My Grinder® Organic Rainbow Peppercorns

4 Hatch Chiles, roasted, peeled, stemmed, seeded, and chopped *(see Hatch Chile Essentials, page 12)*

2 (1.25-pound) pork tenderloins

2½ teaspoons dried basil

2 tablespoons extra-virgin olive oil

1½ cups chicken broth

Preheat the oven to 350°F.

In a saucepan, melt the butter over medium-high heat. Add the mushrooms and garlic to the pan and sauté until the mushrooms are tender. Add the sherry, season with herb salt and pepper, and cook until most of the liquid has evaporated. Stir in the Hatch Chiles and remove the pan from the heat.

Make a deep lengthwise slit down the middle of each of the tenderloins (do not cut all the way through). Stuff the tenderloins with the mushroom filling and tie them closed with butcher's twine. Season the pork on all sides with herb salt and pepper; sprinkle with the basil.

In a large ovenproof skillet, heat the olive oil over high heat until shimmering. Carefully place the tenderloins in the skillet and sear on all sides. Slowly pour the chicken broth into the pan. Cover the pan, transfer it to the oven, and bake until the meat reaches an internal temperature of 150°F to 160°F, about 30 to 40 minutes. Take the tenderloin out of the oven and let it rest for 5 or 10 minutes before slicing.

Note: *To reconstitute dried mushrooms, cover in boiling water or broth and steep for about 20 minutes, then drain the mushrooms, reserving the soaking liquid. Rinse the mushrooms well to remove grit. Strain the flavorful soaking liquid and add to sauces or soup.*

Hatch Chile Skillet Rice

makes 6 servings

¾ pound lean ground pork or lean ground beef

1 onion, chopped

1½ teaspoons Melissa's Hatch Chile Powder

1 teaspoon ground cumin

½ teaspoon salt

3 cups cooked brown rice

1 (16-ounce) can pinto beans, drained

½ cup roasted, peeled, stemmed, seeded, and chopped Hatch Chiles *(see Hatch Chile Essentials, page 12)*

1 fresh tomato, seeded and chopped

1 sprig fresh cilantro, for garnish

Brown the meat in a large nonstick skillet over medium-high heat. Drain off the rendered fat, then add the onions, Hatch Chile powder, cumin and salt to the pan and cook the mixture until the onions are soft but not brown. Stir in the rice, beans, and Hatch Chiles and cook until the mixture is heated through. Top the rice with the tomatoes, garnish with the cilantro, and serve immediately.

Note: *This dish can be made vegetarian by simply eliminating the meat and skipping step one. Use 1 tablespoon of olive oil to saute the onions and spices.*

Baked Chicken
and Yukon Potatoes

makes 6 servings

1 (3-pound) fryer chicken, cut into 8 pieces

Melissa's My Grinder® Organic Garden Herbs with Sea Salt

Melissa's My Grinder® Organic Rainbow Peppercorns

7 tablespoons canola oil, divided

6 Yukon gold potatoes, peeled and quartered

1 cup fresh Roma tomatoes, crushed

4 Hatch Chiles, roasted, peeled, stemmed, and seeded *(see Hatch Chile Essentials, page 12)*

2 tablespoons fresh Italian parsley leaves, chopped

1 teaspoon chopped fresh basil leaves

2 cloves garlic, minced

¼ cup grated Parmesan cheese

Preheat the oven to 375°F. Rinse the chicken pieces under cold running water and pat them dry with paper towels. Season the chicken pieces all over with the herb salt and pepper.

Set a large roasting pan on the stove over medium-high heat. Add 4 tablespoons of the canola oil and heat the pan until the oil shimmers. Carefully add the chicken pieces to the pan and sear the chicken on all sides until golden brown. Add the potatoes and chiles to the pan, using the spaces in between the chicken pieces. Add the tomatoes, chiles, parsley, basil, and garlic to the pan. Season with additional herb salt and pepper. Sprinkle on the cheese and drizzle the remaining 3 tablespoons of canola oil over top the chicken and vegetables. Cover and bake in the oven for 1 hour and 15 minutes, or until the chicken reaches an internal temperature of 170°F.

Hatch Chile Chili

makes 8 servings

2 pounds lean ground beef

1 tablespoon olive oil

1 onion, chopped

1 red onion, chopped

1 cup chopped red bell pepper

8 Hatch Chiles, roasted, peeled, stemmed, seeded, and chopped *(see Hatch Chile Essentials, page 12)*

1 (15-ounce) can tomato sauce

2 packages Melissa's Steamed Ready-to-Eat Red Kidney Beans

1 (28-ounce) can diced tomatoes, with juice

2 teaspoons ground cumin

1½ teaspoons black pepper

Salt

Brown the ground beef in a large saucepan over medium-high heat. Drain off the rendered fat; remove the meat from the pan and set it aside. Add the oil to the saucepan and sauté the onions and bell peppers until translucent, about 5 minutes. Add the chiles and browned ground beef to the pan. Add the tomato sauce, kidney beans, diced tomatoes, cumin, black pepper, and 4 cups of water to the pan. Bring the chili to a boil, then lower heat and simmer until thickened, about 1 hour. Season to taste with salt before serving.

Beef *and* Broccoli

makes 4 to 6 servings

1 tablespoon rice vinegar

1 teaspoon granulated sugar

1 teaspoon plus 2 tablespoons soy sauce

1 tablespoon plus 1 teaspoon cornstarch

¾ pound lean beef, thinly sliced across the grain

⅓ cup green onions, thinly sliced

1 clove garlic, chopped

2 tablespoons oyster sauce

Vegetable oil, for stir-frying

1 pound broccoli, cut into small florets

2 cloves garlic

3 Hatch Chiles, roasted, peeled, stemmed, seeded, and chopped *(see Hatch Chile Essentials, page 12)*

Cooked white rice, for serving

To marinate the beef, combine the rice vinegar, sugar, and 1 teaspoon of the soy sauce in a medium bowl. In a separate small bowl, stir together 1 tablespoon of the cornstarch with 1 tablespoon of water. Add the cornstarch mixture to the soy sauce mixture and mix well, then add the meat, green onions, and garlic. Stir to coat; let marinate for 30 minutes in the refrigerator.

Meanwhile, make the sauce: in a small bowl, combine the oyster sauce with the remaining 2 tablespoons of soy sauce and 1 tablespoon of water. In a separate bowl, mix together the remaining teaspoon of cornstarch with 1 tablespoon water; set aside.

Heat a wok over high heat and add enough oil to coat the pan. Add the marinated beef, season with salt and pepper, and stir-fry for 2 minutes, adding more oil if necessary. Add the broccoli and garlic to the pan and stir-fry for 2 minutes more, then stir in the chiles. Add the sauce, then stir in the cornstarch mixture and cook the beef and broccoli for a final 2 minutes. Serve immediately, over rice.

Hatch Baked Ziti

makes 6 to 8 servings

1 pound uncooked ziti pasta

3 tablespoons extra-virgin olive oil, divided

1 pound lean ground beef

1 Melissa's Perfect Sweet Onion, chopped

3 cloves garlic, minced

1 (28-ounce) can whole tomatoes, crushed with your hands

4 Hatch Chiles, roasted, peeled, stemmed, seeded, and chopped
(see Hatch Chile Essentials, page 12)

1 cup ricotta cheese

3 cups shredded mozzarella cheese

⅓ cup fresh Italian parsley leaves, chopped

¼ cup fresh basil leaves, shredded

½ tablespoon dried oregano

Melissa's My Grinder® Organic Rainbow Peppercorns

¼ cup Italian breadcrumbs

¼ cup grated Parmesan cheese

Cook the pasta al dente as directed on the package.

Meanwhile, preheat the oven to 400°F. Lightly coat a 9 by 12-inch baking dish with 1 tablespoon of the olive oil and set aside.

In a large skillet, heat the remaining 2 tablespoons of olive oil over medium-high heat. Add the onion and ground beef to the pan and sauté until the onions are translucent and the beef is cooked through. Drain the rendered fat from the pan. Add the garlic to the pan and continue sautéing until fragrant, about 30 seconds. Add the tomatoes and chiles, cook for 3 more minutes, then remove the pan from the heat.

In a large bowl, mix the ricotta and mozzarella. Add the parsley, basil, and oregano, season with pepper, and mix well. Add the tomato mixture and stir to combine. Add the cooked pasta and mix well to coat. Transfer the pasta and sauce mixture to the prepared baking dish, sprinkle with the breadcrumbs and Parmesan, and bake until light golden brown, 20 to 30 minutes. Let the pasta rest for 5 minutes before serving.

Note: *Add a little cooked, chopped hot linguiça sausage for kicked-up flavor.*

Creole-Style Black Bean Chili

makes 8 servings

2 tablespoons extra-virgin olive oil

2 tablespoons unsalted butter

1 onion, thinly sliced

2 stalks celery, chopped

1 green bell pepper, diced

1 red bell pepper, diced

2 cloves garlic, minced

2 Hatch Chiles, roasted, peeled, stemmed, seeded, and chopped *(see Hatch Chile Essentials, page 12)*

1 (14-ounce) can diced tomatoes

Kosher salt and black pepper

¼ cup sherry

1 (14-ounce) can vegetable broth

1½ pounds dried black beans, cooked and drained, or 3 (15-ounce) cans black beans, drained

2 chipotle chiles in adobo, minced

1 tablespoon ground cumin

2 teaspoons ground oregano

1 teaspoon ground coriander

2 dried bay leaves

Heat the oil and butter in a large pot over medium heat. Add the onions and cook until caramelized. Stir in the celery, bell peppers, garlic, Hatch Chiles, and tomatoes. Season the mixture with salt and pepper and cook for 5 minutes. Stir in the sherry and cook for an additional 5 minutes, then add the broth, beans, chipotles, cumin, oregano, coriander, and bay leaves. Simmer for 30 minutes. Remove the bay leaves before serving the chili.

Hatch Chicken Alfredo

makes 8 servings

4 boneless, skinless chicken breasts

4 tablespoons olive oil, divided

Melissa's Hatch Chile Powder

Salt

3 tablespoons minced garlic

¼ cup dry white wine

3 cups heavy cream

1 cup roasted, peeled, stemmed, seeded, and chopped Hatch Chiles *(see Hatch Chile Essentials, page 12)*

1 pound uncooked fettuccine

¾ cup grated Parmesan, divided

1 teaspoon fine sea salt

1 teaspoon freshly ground black pepper

½ cup thinly sliced green onion, for garnish

Preheat the oven to 350°F. Bring a large pot of salted water to a boil.

In a large cast-iron skillet, heat 2 tablespoons of the olive oil over high heat until shimmering. Season the chicken with Hatch Chile powder and salt and brown it in the skillet, 2 to 3 minutes per side.

Transfer the chicken to a baking sheet and bake until the internal temperature reaches 165°F on an instant-read thermometer, about 10 minutes. Let cool slightly, then slice into strips on the diagonal.

Heat the cast-iron skillet over medium heat and add the 2 remaining tablespoons of olive oil and the garlic, stirring the garlic for 2 to 3 minutes to lightly brown it. Stir in the wine, then pour in the heavy cream. Bring the mixture to a simmer and cook until the sauce is creamy and reduced by half, 10 to 15 minutes. Add the chiles and the chicken to the sauce, stir to coat, and keep warm.

Meanwhile, cook the fettuccine al dente according to the package directions. Drain.

Add ½ cup of the Parmesan to the sauce and season it with the sea salt and pepper. To serve, toss the pasta with the cream sauce and serve on large rimmed plates. Garnish with the green onions and the remaining ¼ cup Parmesan.

Hatch Chile-Stuffed Meat Loaf

makes 6 servings

1 egg, lightly beaten

1½ cups fresh breadcrumbs

1 cup whole milk

2 tablespoons soy sauce

1 teaspoon Melissa's Hatch Chile Powder

½ cup finely chopped onion

1 pound lean ground beef

1 pound breakfast sausage

4 Hatch Chiles, roasted, peeled, stemmed, seeded, and chopped *(see Hatch Chile Essentials, page 12)*

Melissa's Hatch Salsa Ranchera *(page 157)*, **for serving**

Preheat the oven to 350°F.

In a large bowl, combine the egg, breadcrumbs, milk, soy sauce, chile powder, onion, ground beef, and sausage. Mix lightly, then turn the meat out onto a sheet of wax paper. Cover with another sheet of wax paper and pat the meatloaf mixture into a rectangular shape about ½-inch thick. Lift off the top sheet of wax paper and spread the chopped chiles on the meat in an even layer. Roll the meatloaf up, jellyroll style, into a cylinder. Transfer the meatloaf to a loaf pan or shallow roasting pan and bake for 1½ hours, or until center is cooked through (the juices will run clear when the center of the loaf is pierced with a knife). Serve the meatloaf topped with the salsa.

Hatch Chile *and* Tomatillo Braised Baby Back Ribs

makes 8 servings

3 tablespoons extra-virgin olive oil

4 pounds baby back ribs, silver skin removed *(see Note below)*

Kosher salt and freshly ground black pepper

1 (16-ounce) tub Melissa's Tomatillo Sauce

4 Hatch Chiles, roasted, peeled, stemmed, seeded, and sliced *(see Hatch Chile Essentials, page 12)*

In a large saucepan, heat the oil over high heat. Season the ribs with salt and pepper on all sides and add to the pan. Sear the ribs on all sides until they start to brown. Add the tomatillo sauce and chiles. Cover the pan, lower the heat, and simmer the ribs for 60 to 90 minutes, or until the meat is tender. Remove the lid and simmer for 30 minutes longer. To serve, arrange the ribs on a platter and pour the sauce over the top.

Note: *To remove silver skin from a rack of ribs, slide a thin sharp paring knife under the silver skin anywhere along the rack. If it resists in one spot, try another. Lift and loosen it with the knife until you can grab hold of it with a paper towel. Pull the silver skin off the ribs; it should peel away in one large sheet, but if it breaks, use the knife to restart at another section.*

Hatch Chile Braciole

makes 4 to 6 servings

2 pounds flank steak, trimmed

Kosher salt

Black pepper

½ cup Italian breadcrumbs

½ cup grated Parmesan cheese

½ cup grated mozzarella cheese

1 large egg, lightly beaten

3 Hatch Chiles, roasted, peeled, stemmed, and seeded *(see Hatch Chile Essentials, page 12)*

5 fresh basil leaves

2 tablespoons extra-virgin olive oil

1 (24-ounce) jar prepared pasta sauce

Preheat the oven to 350°F. Use kitchen mallet to pound the flank steak to about ¼-inch thickness. Season the meat with salt and pepper.

In a medium bowl, combine the breadcrumbs, both cheeses, and the egg.

Place the flank steak horizontally on a work surface and spread the breadcrumb mixture onto the bottom third of the flank steak. Layer the chiles and basil leaves on top of the breadcrumb mixture. Starting from the bottom of the long side, roll the steak up tightly and tie it with butcher's twine. Season the meat again with salt and pepper.

In a large ovenproof pan, heat the olive oil over medium-high until shimmering and sear the steak on both sides. Pour the pasta sauce over the steaks and cover the pan with foil. Transfer the pan to the oven and cook for 20 minutes. Remove the foil and cook the steak for an additional 10 minutes or to desired doneness.

Note: *Pounding the flank steak tenderizes it and makes it easy to roll. If you don't have a kitchen mallet, a heavy skillet works just as well.*

Spicy Red Beans *and* Rice with Hatch Chile

makes 6 servings

2 tablespoons olive oil

½ Melissa's Perfect Sweet Onion, finely diced

2 stalks celery, finely diced

4 Hatch Chiles, roasted, peeled, stemmed, seeded, and chopped *(see Hatch Chile Essentials, page 12)*

4 cloves garlic, minced

½ pound cooked hot linguiça sausage, halved lengthwise

½ pound cooked kielbasa sausage, halved lengthwise

1 (12.3-ounce) package Melissa's Steamed Ready-To-Eat Red Kidney Beans, rinsed and drained

2 teaspoons Melissa's Hatch Chile Powder

1 teaspoon dried oregano

1 cup cooked white rice, kept warm

Heat the oil in a large saucepan. Add the onions, celery, chiles, and garlic to the pan. Sauté the mixture over medium-high heat until the onions and the celery are softened. Add the linguiça, kielbasa, kidney beans, chile powder, and dried oregano. Cook until heated through. Stir in the rice and serve.

Hatch Chile Steak Fajitas

makes 4 servings

STEAK

1½ pounds flank steak, trimmed

Freshly squeezed juice of 2 limes

8 cloves garlic, minced

1 (12-ounce) bottle lager, such as Dos Equis

1 teaspoon sea salt

2 teaspoons Melissa's Hatch Chile Powder

1½ teaspoons ground cumin

1½ teaspoons dried oregano

⅓ cup packed brown sugar

4 green onions, ends trimmed

3 Hatch Chiles, roasted, peeled, stemmed, seeded, and chopped *(see Hatch Chile Essentials, page 12)*

⅓ cup extra-virgin olive oil

½ bunch fresh cilantro

VEGETABLES

2 tablespoons extra-virgin olive oil

2 Melissa's Perfect Sweet onions, slivered

3 Hatch Chiles, roasted, peeled, stemmed, seeded, and cut into strips *(see Hatch Chile Essentials, page 13)*

1 red bell pepper, julienned

1 yellow bell pepper, julienned

8 (8-inch) flour tortillas, warmed

To marinate the steak, in a large resealable plastic bag, combine the meat, lime juice, garlic, lager, salt, chile powder, cumin, oregano, brown sugar, green onions, chiles, 1/3 cup olive oil, and cilantro. Seal the bag and shake to mix well. Set the bag in the refrigerator and leave the steak to marinate overnight.

Preheat a grill to high. Transfer the steak to a plate, then grill, turning once, to an internal temperature of 160°F for medium, or to desired doneness. Set the cooked steak aside to rest for 5 minutes before slicing.

Meanwhile, in a sauté pan over medium-high heat, heat 2 tablespoons of olive oil until shimmering. Add the onions to the pan and cook until they are translucent, about 4 minutes. Add the chiles and bell peppers to the pan, season the mixture with salt and pepper, and cook until the bell peppers are tender-crisp, 5 or 6 minutes.

Slice the steak into thin strips and add it to the pepper mixture. Serve the fajitas with warm tortillas.

Hearty Stew

makes 4 servings

½ cup all-purpose flour

2 teaspoons sea salt

¼ teaspoon freshly ground black pepper

3 tablespoons extra-virgin olive oil

4 pounds beef stew meat, cut into 1-inch cubes

4 red boiling onions, peeled and left whole

2 carrots, coarsely chopped

2 turnips, cut into ½-inch cubes

2 parsnips, coarsely chopped

4 Melissa's Baby Dutch Yellow® Potatoes, cut into ½-inch cubes

1 (15-ounce) can stewed tomatoes

5 Hatch Chiles, roasted, peeled, stemmed, seeded, and chopped *(see Hatch Chile Essentials, page 12)*

2½ cups beef broth

2 dried bay leaves

1 tablespoon cornstarch

¾ cup cold water

Whisk together the flour, salt, and pepper in a shallow bowl. Heat the oil in a large pot or Dutch oven over medium-high heat. Dredge the meat in the flour mixture, shaking off the excess flour before placing each piece of meat in the hot oil. Brown the meat on all sides. Add the onions, carrots, turnips, parsnips, and potatoes to the pan. Cook the mixture for 5 minutes, stirring often. Add the tomatoes, chiles, broth, and bay leaves to the pan. Bring the mixture to a boil, then lower the heat to a simmer, cover, and cook until meat is tender, about 45 to 60 minutes.

In a small bowl, mix the cornstarch and water into a smooth slurry. Gradually add the slurry to the stew, stirring constantly (use just enough of the slurry to thicken the stew to your liking). Serve hot.

Note: *A slurry is a mixture of cornstarch and liquid (usually water or broth) used to thicken a sauce or soup. Be careful when adding the cornstarch slurry. If you add too much, your stew may get too thick. To thin it back down, stir in additional hot broth.*

Pork *and* Hatch Chile Verde

makes 4 servings

2 pounds boneless pork shoulder, cut into 1-inch cubes

Salt and black pepper

Vegetable oil

1 large onion, chopped

1½ cups chicken broth

3 cups Tomatillo and Hatch Chile Verde Sauce *(page 152)*

Season the pork with salt and pepper. Heat a large saucepan or skillet over medium-high heat. Add the oil and heat until shimmering. Add the pork and brown on all sides. Transfer the meat to a plate and set aside. Add the onions to the pan and sauté until translucent and softened. Carefully add the chicken broth to the onions, stirring to deglaze the pan. Return the meat to the pan. Add the chile verde sauce and bring the mixture to a boil. Reduce the heat to a simmer. Cover and continue simmering for 35 minutes, or until pork is fork-tender.

Note: *Deglazing is a cooking technique for dissolving the flavor-packed browned bits of food that stick to the bottom of the pan.*

Creamy Étouffée

makes 8 to 10 servings

4 ounces (1 stick) unsalted butter

2 tablespoons canola oil

1 Melissa's Perfect Sweet Onion, finely diced

2 stalks celery, finely diced

1 green bell pepper, finely diced

4 cloves garlic, minced

Sea salt and freshly ground black pepper

4 (10.75-ounce) cans cream of mushroom soup

2 cooked Cajun-style andouille sausages, sliced

4 Hatch Chiles, roasted, peeled, stemmed, seeded, and chopped *(see Hatch Chile Essentials, page 12)*

2 (14.5-ounce) cans diced tomatoes, with juice

Melissa's Hatch Chile Powder

1 pound cooked, peeled, and deveined shrimp, thawed (if frozen) and rinsed

¾ pound langostino tails or crawfish tails, thawed (if frozen) and rinsed

Cooked rice, for serving

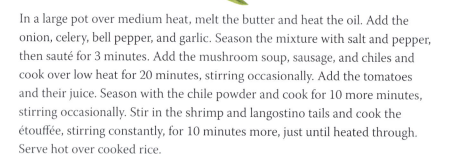

In a large pot over medium heat, melt the butter and heat the oil. Add the onion, celery, bell pepper, and garlic. Season the mixture with salt and pepper, then sauté for 3 minutes. Add the mushroom soup, sausage, and chiles and cook over low heat for 20 minutes, stirring occasionally. Add the tomatoes and their juice. Season with the chile powder and cook for 10 more minutes, stirring occasionally. Stir in the shrimp and langostino tails and cook the étouffée, stirring constantly, for 10 minutes more, just until heated through. Serve hot over cooked rice.

Note: *Langostino (or prawn) tails are similar to the crawfish tails that would be traditional in a Louisiana étouffée; they can be found in the frozen foods section of stores like Trader Joe's and Costco.*

Chicken Chile Empanadas

makes 8 empanadas

1 cup cooked, diced chicken

1 cup shredded Jack cheese

4 Hatch Chiles, roasted, peeled, stemmed, seeded, and chopped *(see Hatch Chile Essentials, page 12)*

1 clove garlic , minced

½ teaspoon ground cumin

1 teaspoon salt

1 (1-pound) package frozen puff pastry, thawed

All-purpose flour, for dusting

1 large egg, beaten

½ teaspoon salt

½ teaspoon freshly ground black pepper

Preheat the oven to 350°F. Lightly coat a large baking sheet with cooking spray.

Mix together the chicken, cheese, Hatch Chiles, garlic, cumin, and salt. Refrigerate the mixture until you are ready to assemble the empanadas, or up to 1 day.

Unfold 1 sheet of puff pastry on a lightly floured surface. Use a lightly floured rolling pin to roll the pastry out to ¼-inch thickness. Use a 5-inch biscuit cutter to cut out 4 circles of dough. Roll and cut the second sheet of pastry the same way.

Spoon 1 tablespoon of the chicken mixture onto the center of each round. Lightly brush the edge of each circle with the beaten egg. Fold the dough over the filling to form a half moon. Crimp the edges with a fork to seal. Transfer the empanadas to the prepared baking sheet and brush them with the remaining egg wash. Bake until golden brown, about 30 minutes. Serve warm.

Garlic-Chile Butter Sautéed Shrimp

makes 6 servings

3 tablespoons unsalted butter, softened

2 jalapeño chiles, finely diced

2 red Fresno chiles, finely diced

3 cloves garlic, roasted and minced

½ teaspoon Melissa's Hatch Chile Powder

2½ cups uncooked white rice

½ cup Tomatillo and Hatch Chile Verde Sauce *(page 152)*

24 large fresh shrimp, peeled and deveined

Fresh cilantro, finely chopped

In a mixing bowl, combine the butter, chiles, garlic, and Hatch Chile powder. Blend the mixture well, form into a log and refrigerate until firm, or up to 3 days.

Combine the rice and 5 cups water in a saucepan. Bring the water to a boil, then reduce the heat to low, cover, and simmer for 18 to 20 minutes, or until the rice is tender. Mix the Tomatillo and Hatch Chile Verde Sauce into the cooked rice and cover the pot to keep warm.

Melt the garlic-chile butter in a sauté pan over medium-high heat. Add the shrimp and cook, stirring often, until shrimp turns pink and opaque. This will only take a couple of minutes.

To serve, spread the rice on a platter and lay the shrimp decoratively over top. Drizzle some of the butter from the pan over the shrimp, if desired. Garnish with cilantro.

Note: *This dish pairs beautifully with a chilled bottle of Fumé Blanc.*

Picadillo

makes 4 servings

¼ cup raisins

1 pound lean ground beef

½ onion, sliced

1 tablespoon olive oil

4 cloves garlic, chopped

4 tomatoes, seeded and diced

8 green olives, pitted and quartered

2 Hatch Chiles, roasted, peeled, stemmed, seeded, and chopped
(see Hatch Chile Essentials, page 12)

1 teaspoon ground cumin

1 teaspoon brown sugar

2 potatoes, peeled and cubed

Put the raisins in a small bowl, cover with warm water, and leave to soak until softened, about 20 minutes.

Cook the ground beef and onions in the olive oil in a large skillet over medium heat, stirring to crumble the beef and cooking until the beef is about halfway done (with some pink remaining). Add the garlic to the pan and continue cooking the mixture for 2 more minutes, stirring often. Add the tomatoes, olives, chiles, cumin, brown sugar, potatoes, and 1½ cups of water. Stir to combine, then lower the heat to low and simmer the picadillo until the beef is well browned and crumbly and the potatoes are fully cooked, 10 to 12 minutes.

Note: *Picadillo is a rich ground beef dish that is often served over rice or used as a filling for tamales, empanadas, and tacos.*

Green Chile Meat Stew

makes 6 servings

3 pounds beef chuck, cut into 1-inch pieces

½ teaspoon black pepper

2 teaspoons salt

2 tablespoons vegetable oil

2 large white onions, chopped

3 cloves garlic, minced

1 tablespoon ground cumin

1 (28-ounce) can whole tomatoes, with juice

12 Hatch Chiles, roasted, peeled, stemmed, seeded, and cut lengthwise into ⅓-inch-wide strips *(see Hatch Chile Essentials, page 12)*

Cooked rice, for serving

Season the meat with the salt and pepper. Heat the oil in a heavy large pot over moderately high heat until hot but not smoking. Cook the beef in 2 or 3 batches, turning occasionally, until browned, 6 to 8 minutes per batch. Transfer the batches of browned meat to a bowl and reserve.

Add the onion and garlic to the beef drippings and cook over moderately high heat, stirring and scraping up the brown bits, until the onions have softened, about 8 minutes. Add the cumin and cook, stirring, 2 minutes more. Return the beef and any accumulated juices to the pot, then stir in the tomatoes. Add 2 cups water and bring the stew to a simmer. Add the chiles and continue to simmer gently, uncovered, stirring occasionally to break up the tomatoes, until the meat is very tender, about 3 hours. Serve over rice.

Meatballs

makes 4 to 5 servings

Vegetable oil or cooking spray

½ pound ground pork

1 pound lean ground beef

4 Hatch Chiles, roasted, peeled, stemmed, seeded, and chopped *(see Hatch Chile Essentials, page 12)*

½ cup finely grated cheddar cheese

1 large egg

1½ teaspoons dried oregano

1 teaspoon garlic powder

1 teaspoon kosher salt

1 teaspoon Melissa's Hatch Chile Powder

½ cup dry breadcrumbs, divided

Tomatillo and Hatch Chile Verde Sauce *(page 152)*, for serving

Preheat the oven to 400°F. Lightly coat a baking sheet with oil or cooking spray.

In a large mixing bowl, combine the ground meats, chiles, cheese, egg, oregano, garlic powder, salt, chile powder, and ¼ cup of the breadcrumbs. Use your hands to mix until well incorporated.

Place the remaining ¼ cup of breadcrumbs in a small bowl.

Portion out 20 meatballs, rolling each meatball with your hands to shape, then rolling it through the breadcrumbs to coat and setting it on the prepared baking sheet.

Bake the meatballs for 20 minutes or until golden and cooked through. Serve with the chile sauce.

HATCH CHILE

CASSEROLES
&SOUPS

Crab *and* Grilled Corn Chowder

makes 12 servings

4 ears corn, husks and silk removed

4 tablespoons plus 4 ounces (1 stick) unsalted butter, divided

½ pound bacon, finely diced

1 Melissa's Perfect Sweet onion, finely diced

8 cloves garlic, minced

4 shallots, minced

2 stalks celery, diced

1 cup all-purpose flour

4 cups whole milk

2 cups heavy cream

2 dried bay leaves

2 large Yukon gold potatoes, peeled and diced

4 Hatch Chiles, roasted, peeled, stemmed, seeded, and chopped *(see Hatch Chile Essentials, page 12)*

1 pound fresh crabmeat

Salt and black pepper

Preheat a grill to medium-high.

Melt 4 tablespoons of the butter and brush it on the corn. Season the corn with salt and pepper and grill until slightly charred. Remove the corn from the heat. When it is cool enough to handle, cut the kernels from the cob and set them aside.

Heat a large stockpot over medium heat and sauté the bacon until it is crisp. Next add the onions, garlic, shallots, and celery. Cook the mixture for 5 minutes. Add the stick of butter and heat until melted. Stir in the flour and cook, stirring constantly with a whisk until smooth, about 3 minutes. Whisk in the milk and cream. Next add the bay leaves, potatoes, and chiles. Bring the chowder to a boil. Lower the heat to a simmer, then cover and cook until potatoes are tender.

Remove and discard the bay leaves and stir in the crabmeat and the reserved corn. Taste and adjust seasonings. Serve hot.

Note: *This chowder is great with garlic bread.*

Hatch *and* Chayote Casserole

makes 8 servings

Cooking spray

5 chayotes, peeled, pitted, and cut into ¾-inch cubes

2 tablespoons vegetable oil, divided

1 small onion, sliced crosswise into ⅛-inch thick rounds

2 cloves garlic, minced

¼ teaspoon dried oregano

¼ teaspoon dried thyme

3 Hatch Chiles, roasted, peeled, stemmed, seeded, and sliced
(see Hatch Chile Essentials, page 12)

1½ cups corn kernels

⅔ cup whole milk

1 teaspoon salt

1 cup shredded Jack cheese, divided

¾ cup breadcrumbs

⅓ cup grated Parmesan cheese

Preheat the oven to 350°F. Lightly coat a 9-inch square baking pan with cooking spray.

In a steamer, cook the chayote about 15 minutes, or until tender. Set aside.

In a sauté pan over medium-high heat, cook the onion in 1 tablespoon of the oil for 5 minutes. Add the garlic, herbs, and chiles. Stir the mixture to combine thoroughly, then stir in the corn, milk, and chayote. Bring the mixture to a boil. Season with the salt.

Spoon half of the chayote mixture into the prepared baking pan. Top with ½ cup of the Jack cheese. Layer in the rest of the chayote mixture, followed by the remaining ½ cup of Jack cheese. Bake the casserole for 20 minutes.

In a small bowl, combine the breadcrumbs and the Parmesan and stir in the remaining tablespoon of oil. Sprinkle the breadcrumb mixture over casserole and bake it for 15 more minutes.

Hatch Chile Mexican Pasta Casserole

makes 6 to 8 servings

Cooking spray

1 pound uncooked penne or other medium-size pasta shape

2 teaspoons vegetable oil

1 onion, chopped

1 clove garlic, minced

2 Hatch Chiles, roasted, peeled, stemmed, seeded, and chopped *(see Hatch Chile Essentials, page 12)*

3 tablespoons Melissa's Hatch Chile Powder

1 (28-ounce) can diced tomatoes, with juice

1 teaspoon ground cumin

1 teaspoon dried oregano

8 ounces cooked boneless, skinless chicken breast, cubed

1 cup shredded Jack cheese, divided

Preheat the oven to 375°F. Lightly coat a 2-quart baking dish with cooking spray.

Prepare pasta according to package directions.

While the pasta is cooking, heat the oil in a medium saucepan over medium heat. Add the onions, garlic, and chiles, and cook until the onion has softened, about 3 minutes. Add the chile powder and stir for 1 minute. Add the tomatoes and their liquid, then stir in the cumin and oregano. Simmer the sauce until slightly thickened, about 15 minutes.

Drain the pasta well. In a bowl, combine the pasta, sauce, chicken, and ¾ cup of the Jack cheese. Mix well and spoon into the prepared baking dish. Sprinkle the remaining ¼ cup of cheese on top. Cover the casserole loosely with foil and bake until it is warmed through and the cheese has melted, about 15 minutes.

Baby Cauliflower *and* Potato Cheese Soup

makes 6 to 8 servings

3 tablespoons extra-virgin olive oil

1 tablespoon unsalted butter

2 Melissa's Perfect Sweet Onions, chopped

2 cloves garlic, chopped

1 stalk celery, chopped

4 teaspoons fresh dill

2 teaspoons fresh thyme leaves

8 heads white baby cauliflower, chopped

6 cups chicken broth

4 cups diced Melissa's Baby Dutch Yellow® Potatoes

3 Hatch Chiles, roasted, peeled, stemmed, seeded, and chopped *(see Hatch Chile Essentials, page 12)*

4 fresh bay leaves

1 cup heavy cream

½ cup shredded fresh Parmesan cheese

2 heads green baby cauliflower, cut into small florets

2 heads orange baby cauliflower, cut into small florets

Melissa's My Grinder® Organic Garden Herbs with Sea Salt

Melissa's My Grinder® Organic Rainbow Peppercorns

In a medium soup pot, heat the oil and butter over medium heat. Sauté the onions until they are translucent, then add the garlic and cook just until it is aromatic, about 30 seconds. Add the celery, herbs, and white cauliflower and cook for 5 minutes, stirring often. Next add the chicken broth, potatoes, chiles, and bay leaves. Bring to a boil, lower the heat to a simmer, and cover and cook the soup for 30 minutes.

Remove and discard the bay leaves. Take the pot off of the heat and carefully purée the soup with a hand blender until smooth.

Return the pot to the stove, bring back to a simmer, and stir in the cream and the Parmesan. Cook gently until the cheese melts, then stir in green and orange cauliflower florets and season to taste with the herb salt and rainbow pepper. The florets will cook just slightly from the warmth of the soup.

Chile Relleno Casserole

makes 6 servings

Vegetable oil

8 Hatch Chiles, roasted, peeled, stemmed, seeded, and left whole
(see Hatch Chile Essentials, page 12)

4 cups shredded mozzarella cheese

4 large eggs

1½ cups whole milk

2 tablespoons all-purpose flour

½ teaspoon black pepper

¼ teaspoon kosher salt

Melissa's Hatch Chile Powder

Green onions, sliced for garnish

Preheat the oven to 350°F. Lightly oil a baking dish.

Lay 4 of the chiles in a single layer in the bottom of the baking dish. Sprinkle with half of the mozzarella. Repeat with the remaining chiles and the remaining cheese. In a mixing bowl, whisk together the eggs, milk, flour, salt, and pepper until well blended and frothy. Pour the egg mixture over the chiles and cheese. Sprinkle the top with the Hatch powder.

Bake the casserole until the eggs have set and a knife inserted into the center of the casserole comes out clean, about 45 minutes. Let stand, uncovered, for about 20 minutes before serving. Garnish with sliced green onions.

Hatch Chile
and Tatuma Squash Soup

makes 6 servings

2 tablespoons vegetable oil

1 onion, chopped

5 cups sliced Tatuma squash
(see Note, page 87)

2 cloves garlic, minced

1 (28-ounce) can tomatoes,
with juice

2 cups fresh corn kernels, cooked
and drained

8 Hatch Chiles, roasted, peeled,
stemmed, seeded, and chopped
(see Hatch Chile Essentials, page 12)

½ teaspoon ground cumin

1 teaspoon Melissa's Hatch
Chile Powder

1 (12-ounce) can evaporated milk

Salt

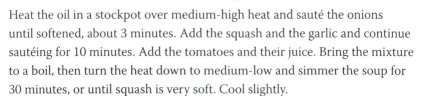

Heat the oil in a stockpot over medium-high heat and sauté the onions
until softened, about 3 minutes. Add the squash and the garlic and continue
sautéing for 10 minutes. Add the tomatoes and their juice. Bring the mixture
to a boil, then turn the heat down to medium-low and simmer the soup for
30 minutes, or until squash is very soft. Cool slightly.

Working in small batches, purée the soup in a blender until smooth.
Return the soup to the pot and stir in the corn, chiles, cumin, and chile powder.
Reheat the soup, stirring in the milk and seasoning with salt to taste.

Hatch Chile Chowder

makes 6 servings

2 tablespoons olive oil

1 large onion, minced

3 cups fresh corn kernels, divided

3 cups whole milk, divided

1 large russet potato (about 1 pound), peeled and diced

1 teaspoon salt

½ cup heavy cream

4 Hatch Chiles, roasted, peeled, stemmed, seeded, and chopped
(see Hatch Chile Essentials, page 12)

Salt and black pepper

Heat the olive oil over medium heat in a saucepan and cook the onion until it is soft and translucent, about 5 minutes. In a blender, purée 1 cup of the corn with 1 cup of the milk. Pour the corn purée into the pan and add the remaining 2 cups corn and 2 cups milk, along with the potatoes and 1 teaspoon of salt. Reduce the heat and simmer the chowder 10 to 15 minutes, or until the potatoes are fork-tender. Stir in the cream and the Hatch Chiles. Season with salt and pepper.

Baked Potato Soup

makes 4 servings

2 potatoes, baked and cooled

3 cups chicken broth

4 tablespoons sour cream

¼ teaspoon black pepper

2 Hatch Chiles, roasted, peeled, stemmed, seeded, and chopped
(see Hatch Chile Essentials, page 12)

Salt

½ cup shredded cheddar cheese

Peel the potatoes, cut them into ½-inch cubes, and set half of them aside. Combine the remaining potato cubes in a blender with the chicken broth and process until smooth. Pour the mixture into a saucepan. Stir in the sour cream, black pepper, chiles, and reserved potato cubes. Cook the soup over low heat until heated through (do not boil). Season to taste with salt. Garnish with the cheese and serve hot.

Hatch Chile Albóndigas Soup

makes 8 servings

MEATBALLS

1 pound lean ground beef

½ cup dry Italian breadcrumbs

¼ cup grated Parmesan cheese

1 Melissa's Perfect Sweet Onion, chopped

2 cloves garlic, minced

Melissa's My Grinder® Organic Garlic & Herbs with Sea Salt

Melissa's My Grinder® Organic Rainbow Peppercorns

Cold water, as needed

2 tablespoons extra-virgin olive oil

SOUP

3 quarts beef broth

1 (28-ounce) can whole tomatoes, chopped, with juice

½ cup Hatch Chile, roasted, peeled, stemmed, seeded, and chopped *(see Hatch Chile Essentials, page 12)*

1 Melissa's Perfect Sweet Onion, diced

1½ teaspoons crushed dried basil

1½ teaspoons crushed dried oregano

1 teaspoon Tabasco® sauce

½ cup long-grain white rice

½ cup minced fresh cilantro

Salt and black pepper

To make the meatballs, combine the beef, breadcrumbs, Parmesan, onions, garlic, herb salt, and pepper in a large bowl. Slowly add cold water in small amounts, stirring well, until the mixture is moist but not wet. Use your hands to form the mixture into 15 to 20 small balls. Heat the olive oil in a skillet and brown the meatballs on all sides.

In a large stockpot, combine the beef broth, tomatoes and their liquid, chiles, onions, basil, oregano, and Tabasco. Bring to a boil over high heat. Add the rice, then lower the heat, cover, and simmer for 15 minutes. Add the meatballs, then cover and cook an additional 10 minutes, or until the meatballs are cooked through. Stir in the cilantro and season the soup to taste with salt and pepper.

Enchiladas Verde

½ cups cooked, shredded chicken

4 Hatch Chiles, roasted, peeled, stemmed, seeded, and chopped *(see Hatch Chile Essentials, page 12)*

1½ cups shredded mild white cheese (panela, Jack, mozzarella, or queso blanco)

3 cups Tomatillo and Hatch Chile Verde Sauce *(page 152)*, divided

12 corn tortillas

Vegetable oil

¼ cup crumbled Cotija cheese

Toss together the chicken, chiles, shredded cheese, and 1 cup of the chile sauce. Set aside.

In a small skillet, heat ½ inch of oil over medium-high heat until shimmering. Briefly warm each tortilla in the oil to soften.

Lay a tortilla flat and fill it with about ¼ cup of filling down the center. Bring the edges together over the filling to close, then set the tortilla seam-side down in a 9 x 13-inch baking dish. Repeat until all the tortillas are filled. Pour the remaining 2 cups of sauce over the top. Sprinkle with the Cotija cheese. Bake for 20 minutes at 300°F.

Mango-Hatch Rellenos
with Mango-Chipotle Sauce

makes 6 servings

6 fresh Hatch Chiles, roasted, peeled, and left whole *(see Hatch Chile Essentials, page 12)*

2 ripe mangoes, divided

1½ cups shredded Jack cheese

2 chipotle chiles in adobo sauce

1 pinch kosher salt

Preheat the oven to broil.

Make a lengthwise slit down the side of each Hatch Chile, taking care not to cut through the tip. Carefully remove the seeds.

Peel, pit, and dice one of the mangos. In a small bowl, mix the diced mango with the cheese. Stuff the peppers with the mango-cheese mixture and set them under the broiler. Cook until the cheese is melted and the peppers are heated through.

Peel, pit, and dice the remaining mango and combine it in a blender with the chipotle chiles, salt, and 1 tablespoon of water. Blend into a smooth sauce.

To serve, place one stuffed Hatch Chile on each of six plates and garnish with the sauce.

Note: *This recipe would also be great with cheddar cheese or a combination of Jack and cheddar.*

Vegetable Soup

makes 4 to 6 servings

2 tablespoons extra-virgin olive oil

2 tablespoons unsalted butter

1 Melissa's Perfect Sweet Onion, julienned

2 cups diced carrots

1 cup diced celery

3 cloves garlic, minced

Melissa's My Grinder® Organic Garden Herbs with Sea Salt

Melissa's My Grinder® Organic Rainbow Peppercorns

Melissa's My Grinder® Organic Italian Seasoning

6 cups chicken broth

1 (14-ounce) can crushed tomatoes, with juice

4 Hatch Chiles, roasted, peeled, stemmed, seeded, and chopped *(see Hatch Chile Essentials, page 12)*

1½ cups diced zucchini

1½ cups diced yellow squash

2 large sprigs fresh thyme

4 tablespoons chopped fresh Italian parsley

In a large stockpot, heat the oil and butter and sauté the onions until translucent. Add the carrots and celery and continue to cook until they are tender-crisp. Next, add the garlic and season with the herb salt, pepper, and Italian seasoning. Once the garlic is fragrant, less than a minute, add the chicken broth, tomatoes, chiles, zucchini, yellow squash, thyme, and parsley. Bring the soup to a boil, then lower the heat and simmer for about 30 minutes, to allow the flavors to incorporate. Remove the thyme sprigs before serving.

Red Beans *and* Farro-Stuffed Hatch Chiles

makes 6 servings

1 package Melissa's Organic Farro, rinsed

3 chipotle chiles

3 dried chiles de árbol

1 (3-ounce) package Melissa's Roasted Sweet Corn

½ pound sweet Italian sausage, chopped

½ pound spicy Italian sausage, chopped

2 tablespoons extra-virgin olive oil

1 Melissa's Perfect Sweet Onion, finely diced

1 green bell pepper, finely diced

2 stalks celery, finely diced

1 serrano chile, sliced into rounds

4 cloves garlic, minced

4 Melissa's Pimientos Del Piquillo, drained and finely diced

1 package Melissa's Steamed Ready-to-Eat Red Kidney Beans, rinsed

⅛ teaspoon Melissa's Hatch Chile Powder

1 teaspoon dried oregano

Sea salt

6 large Hatch Chiles, roasted, peeled, and left whole *(see Hatch Chile Essentials, page 12)*

Combine the farro with the chipotle and de árbol chiles in a saucepan and prepare according to the farro package instructions.

Put the dried sweet corn in a large heatproof bowl and cover with hot water to rehydrate. Soak until tender, about 20 minutes; drain thoroughly and set aside.

Preheat the oven to 350°F.

Heat a large pan on the stove and cook the sausages until done through. Remove them from the pan and set aside. Add the olive oil, onion, bell pepper, celery, serrano chile, and garlic to the pan and cook them over medium-high heat until the vegetables soften and release their moisture, about 5 minutes. Return the cooked sausages to the pan, and add the cooked farro and rehydrated corn as well as the pimientos, beans, chile powder, and oregano. Season with the salt and cook until heated through. Keep warm.

To stuff the Hatch Chiles, make a lengthwise slit down the side of each pepper, taking care not to cut through the tip. Carefully remove and discard the seeds, then stuff the chiles with the warm farro mixture (do not overfill). Heat the chiles on a baking sheet in the oven for 5 minutes before serving.

Note: *Serve with your favorite sauce or salsa.*

Green Chile Soup

makes 4 servings

¼ cup vegetable oil

1 pound beef round steak

¼ cup all-purpose flour

1 onion, chopped

2 cups beef broth

6 Hatch Chiles, roasted, peeled, stemmed, seeded, and chopped *(see Hatch Chile Essentials, page 12)*

4 cups fresh or canned chopped tomatoes, drained

¼ teaspoon Melissa's Hatch Chile Powder

¼ teaspoon dried oregano

Salt and pepper

Heat the oil over medium heat in large pot. Dredge the meat in the flour and brown it on all sides. Add onions to the pan and cook until onions are translucent. Add the broth, chiles, tomatoes, chile powder, and oregano. Season with salt and pepper and simmer, covered, for about 1 hour.

Chiles Rellenos

makes 6 servings

12 large Hatch Chiles, roasted, peeled, and left whole *(see Hatch Chile Essentials, page 12)*

1 pound cheddar, Jack, or queso blanco cheese, shredded

4 large eggs, well chilled and separated

4 tablespoons all-purpose flour

¾ teaspoon baking soda

¼ teaspoon salt

1 cup vegetable oil

Melissa's Hatch Salsa Ranchera, for serving *(page 157)*

Slit the chiles lengthwise and remove the seeds. Stuff with the cheese, using toothpicks to hold the chiles closed.

In a large bowl, beat the egg whites with an electric mixer until soft peaks form. Add the flour, baking soda, salt, and the yolks and mix until completely incorporated.

Heat the oil to 350°F in a large deep skillet over medium heat. Working in batches, dip the stuffed peppers into the batter and fry, turning once, until golden brown, about 3 minutes per side. Drain on paper towels.

Serve the chiles with Melissa's Hatch Salsa Ranchera (page 157).

Spicy Hatch Tropical Fruit Salsa

Spicy Hatch Tropical Fruit Salsa

makes 5 to 6 cups

1 cup diced strawberry papaya or red papaya

1 cup diced mango

1 cup diced South African baby pineapple or golden pineapple

1 red onion, diced

1 Hatch Chile, roasted, peeled, stemmed, seeded, and chopped
(see Hatch Chile Essentials, page 12)

½ bunch fresh cilantro, chopped

½ jicama, peeled and diced

Freshly squeezed juice of 2 Valencia oranges

Freshly squeezed juice of 6 Key limes

Salt and black pepper

In a large mixing bowl, combine the papaya, mango, pineapple, onions, chiles, cilantro, jicama, and citrus juices. Stir gently to combine and season to taste with salt and pepper. Chill before serving, up to 24 hours.

Hatch Chile Salad Dressing

makes 1⅓ cups

1 tablespoon Melissa's Hatch Chile Powder

2 Hatch Chiles, roasted, peeled, stemmed, seeded, and chopped
(see Hatch Chile Essentials, page 12)

½ cup ketchup

¾ cup vinegar

1 tablespoon oil

1 teaspoon granulated sugar

2 cloves garlic, minced

Salt and freshly ground black pepper

Combine the chile powder, chiles, ketchup, vinegar, oil, sugar, and garlic in a bowl. Mix well and season to taste with salt and pepper. Refrigerate for at least 1 hour before serving.

Note: *Use as a salad dressing or dipping sauce.*

Hatch Chile Jelly

makes 10 half-pint jars

2 pounds Hatch Chiles, roasted, peeled, stemmed, and seeded
(see Hatch Chile Essentials, page 12)

4 cups cider vinegar

12 cups granulated sugar

4 (3-ounce) pouches liquid pectin

Working in batches if necessary, combine the chile and the vinegar in blender and purée to a coarse texture, leaving some small bits of chile. Combine the chile vinegar with the sugar in large saucepan and set over high heat. Bring to a boil, and then lower the heat to maintain a steady boil. Cook, stirring constantly, for 20 minutes. Stir in the liquid pectin and return to a boil, stirring constantly. Continue boiling and stirring until the mixture reaches a jell state (220°F on a candy thermometer, or thickened to the point where it "sheets," rather than drips, off of a large metal spoon held about 18 inches above the pan).

Can the hot jelly in standard canning jars according to jar manufacturer's instructions.

Hatch Chile Mayonnaise

makes 1½ cups

1 cup good-quality mayonnaise

1 teaspoon minced garlic

1 Hatch Chile, roasted, peeled, stemmed, seeded, and chopped *(see Hatch Chile Essentials, page 12)*

1 tablespoon fresh lime juice

Salt and freshly ground black pepper

Combine the mayonnaise, garlic, chiles, and lime juice in the bowl of a food processor. Process until smooth. Season to taste with salt and pepper.

Note: *Use as a dip for vegetables or a spread for sandwiches or burgers.*

Quick Hatch Chile Salsa Fresca

makes 3 cups

2 cups diced Roma tomatoes

½ red onion, diced

1½ Hatch Chiles, roasted, peeled, stemmed, seeded, and chopped
(see Hatch Chile Essentials, page 12)

½ bunch fresh cilantro, chopped

Freshly squeezed juice of 2 Key limes

Melissa's My Grinder® Organic Garlic & Herbs with Sea Salt

Melissa's My Grinder® Organic Rainbow Peppercorns

Mix the tomatoes, onions, chiles, cilantro, and lime juice together in a bowl. Season to taste with salt and pepper. Chill at least 1 hour or up to 2 days. Serve with chips or as desired.

Will keep in refrigerator up to 2 days.

Roasted Hatch *and* Tomatillo Salsa

makes about 2 cups

1 pound fresh tomatillos

3 fresh Hatch Chiles, halved lengthwise *(see Hatch Chile Essentials, page 12)*

3 red Fresno peppers, halved lengthwise

1 Melissa's Perfect Sweet Onion, quartered

Extra-virgin olive oil

Salt and black pepper

1 tomato, quartered

2 cloves garlic

Freshly squeezed juice of 1 Meyer lemon

Freshly squeezed juice of 2 Key limes

½ bunch fresh cilantro, chopped

1 pinch Melissa's Hatch Chile Powder

Preheat the oven to 425°F. Peel off and discard the husks of the tomatillos. Rinse the tomatillos under cold running water.

Put the tomatillos, Hatch Chiles, peppers, and onions on a baking sheet. Drizzle the vegetables with the olive oil, season with salt and pepper, then roast in the oven until slightly charred, 10 to 15 minutes.

In a blender, combine the roasted vegetables with the tomato, garlic, lemon and lime juice, cilantro, and chile powder. Carefully purée the mixture to desired consistency. Adjust seasonings to taste with additional salt, pepper, and Hatch Chile powder.

Tomatillo *and* Hatch Chile Verde Sauce

makes 3 cups

1 tablespoon olive oil

½ onion, chopped

3 cloves garlic, minced

6 Hatch Chiles, roasted, peeled, stemmed, seeded, and chopped *(see Hatch Chile Essentials, page 12)*

1 cup chicken broth

½ teaspoon salt

½ teaspoon ground cumin

1 (16-ounce) tub Melissa's Tomatillo Sauce

Heat the oil over in a skillet over medium-high heat. Add the onion and sauté until translucent and soft. Add the garlic and sauté 1 minute without allowing the garlic to brown. Add chiles, chicken broth, salt, and cumin. Bring the mixture to a boil, then lower heat and simmer for 15 minutes. Let cool slightly.

Combine the chile mixture and the tomatillo sauce in a blender and purée.

Note: *This sauce is incredibly versatile. It makes a great dip for chips and a marvelous sauce for many dishes, such as tacos, chilaquiles (page 21), enchiladas (page 140), pork (page 123), shrimp (page 126), and meatballs (page 129).*

Black Bean
and Pineapple Salsa

makes 5 cups

1 (15-ounce) can black beans, rinsed and drained

1 small pineapple, peeled and chopped

2 Hatch Chiles, roasted, peeled, stemmed, seeded, and chopped *(see Hatch Chile Essentials, page 12)*

2 plum tomatoes, seeded, chopped

4 green onions, chopped

¼ cup prepared Italian vinaigrette salad dressing

1 tablespoon freshly squeezed lime juice

2 teaspoons chopped fresh cilantro

½ teaspoon garlic salt

1 teaspoon Melissa's Hatch Chile Powder

Tortilla chips, for serving

Combine the beans, pineapple, chiles, tomatoes, green onions, dressing, lime juice, cilantro, garlic salt, and chile powder in a medium bowl. Stir to combine. Cover and chill the salsa at least 1 hour, or up to 24 hours. Serve with tortilla chips.

Chef Tom's Southern California Black-Eyed Pea Relish

makes about 6 cups

½ red onion, diced

1 yellow bell pepper, diced

1 red bell pepper, diced

1 green bell pepper, diced

3 Hatch Chiles, roasted, peeled, stemmed, seeded, and chopped *(see Hatch Chile Essentials, page 12)*

2 cloves garlic, minced

1 Roma tomato, diced

2 (11-ounce) packages Melissa's Steamed Ready-to-Eat Black-Eyed Peas, rinsed and drained

¼ cup seasoned rice vinegar

Sea salt and freshly ground black pepper

In a bowl, gently combine all of the ingredients. Refrigerate for 1 hour to incorporate flavors.

Note: *Try this dish with some chips for a great New Year's Day appetizer. According to various traditions, eating black-eyed peas brings good fortune in the new year.*

Red Chile Sauce

makes 2 cups

2 tablespoons olive oil

1 small onion, finely chopped

1 clove garlic, minced

2 tablespoons all-purpose flour

1 cup Melissa's Hatch Chile Powder

¼ teaspoon ground cumin

1 (8-ounce) can tomato sauce

½ teaspoon salt

Sauté the onions and garlic in the oil until they are slightly browned. Add the flour and continue to cook for 4 minutes, stirring constantly until the flour is browned, being careful that it does not scorch. Stir in the Hatch Chile powder and cumin and heat for a couple of minutes. Add the tomato sauce and 6½ cups water, bring to a boil, reduce the heat, and simmer for 10 to 15 minutes, or until the sauce has thickened as desired. Season with salt to taste. For a smoother consistency, let the sauce cool and purée it in a blender.

Note: *Use as an enchilada sauce or in any recipe that calls for red chile sauce.*

Melissa's Hatch Salsa Ranchera

makes 4 cups

1 tablespoon olive oil

1 large onion, chopped

2 cloves garlic, minced

8 Hatch Chiles, roasted, peeled, stemmed, seeded, and sliced into thin strips *(see Hatch Chile Essentials, page 12)*

1 (28-ounce) can diced tomatoes, with juice

¼ teaspoon ground cumin

¼ teaspoon salt

1 tablespoon cornstarch

1 cup chicken broth

Heat the olive oil in a large sauté pan over medium-high heat. Add the onions and sauté until translucent and softened. Add the garlic to the pan and sauté 1 minute, without allowing the garlic to brown. Add the chiles to the pan and sauté the mixture for 3 more minutes. Stir in the tomatoes and their juice, then add the cumin and salt. Bring the mixture to a boil, then lower the heat and let simmer for 15 minutes.

Meanwhile, dissolve the cornstarch in the chicken broth. Add the broth mixture to the pan and bring the salsa to a boil. Lower the heat to a simmer and cook the salsa for 10 minutes or until thickened as desired.

Avocado Mango Salsa

makes 1½ cups

1 Ataulfo mango, diced
(see Note below)

1 avocado, diced

1 fresh Hatch Chile, seeded
and diced *(see Hatch Chile Essentials,
page 12)*

½ cup finely diced red onion,
soaked in cold water for 10 minutes
and drained

3 tablespoons fresh cilantro leaves,
finely chopped

2 tablespoons freshly squeezed
lime juice

2 tablespoons freshly squeezed
orange juice

Kosher salt and freshly ground
black pepper

Combine the mango, avocado, chile, onion, cilantro, and citrus juices in a bowl.
Toss gently to mix. Season to taste with salt and pepper and serve immediately.

Note: *The mango should be only slightly soft to touch; any softer and it will be
overripe, quickly losing its shape and dissolving into the salsa. This refreshing
salsa is great with grilled fish.*

HATCH CHILE
DESSERTS & DRINKS

Hatch Chile *and* Vanilla Bean Ice Cream

makes about 1 quart

4 egg yolks

2 cups whole milk

1 cup heavy cream

¾ cup granulated sugar, divided

2 vanilla beans, split lengthwise

8 Hatch Chiles, roasted, peeled, stemmed, seeded, and diced, divided *(see Hatch Chile Essentials, page 12)*

½ teaspoon vanilla extract

In a small bowl, whip the egg yolks with ¼ cup of the sugar until smooth. In a large saucepan, combine the milk, cream, the remaining ½ cup of sugar, vanilla beans, and half of the Hatch Chiles. Set the saucepan over medium-high heat and heat, stirring constantly, to just below boiling. Pour some of the hot milk mixture into the egg mixture to temper the eggs. Mix well, and then add the egg mixture to the sauce pan and cook over low heat, stirring often with a wooden spoon, until it is thick enough to coat the back of the spoon.

Strain the custard into a bowl and stir in the vanilla extract. Cover the bowl and set it in the refrigerator until thoroughly chilled, 4 to 6 hours.

Add the remaining Hatch Chiles to the chilled custard and stir to incorporate. Transfer the custard to an ice cream maker and freeze according to the manufacturer's instructions.

Hatch Chile S'mores

makes 10 s'mores

5 graham crackers, snapped along perforations into quarters

40 miniature marshmallows

12 ounces semisweet chocolate chips

2 tablespoons vegetable oil

½ teaspoon Melissa's Hatch Chile Powder

Preheat the oven to 350°F.

On a baking sheet, spread half of the cracker quarters. Top each with 4 marshmallows and bake until the marshmallows begin to melt, about 5 minutes. Take the crackers out of the oven and immediately top them with the remaining cracker quarters, pressing down slightly.

Combine the chocolate and oil in a microwave-safe bowl. Microwave on high for 1 minute, then stir the mixture with a wooden spoon. Continue microwaving on high in 10-second increments, stirring well after each increment, until the chocolate and oil are completely melted, combined, and smooth. Add the chile powder to the chocolate and stir to incorporate. Dip each cracker sandwich into the melted chocolate, turning to coat all sides and setting on parchment paper to dry.

Note: *This is a fun treat with a little punch. Make sure the bowl and the spoon you use for melting the chocolate are both perfectly dry, as any moisture can cause the chocolate to seize (form a hard grainy mass) rather than melt smoothly.*

Hatch Peanut Brittle

makes 1 pound candy

1 cup granulated sugar

½ cup light corn syrup

¼ teaspoon salt

1 cup peanuts

½ cup roasted, peeled, stemmed, seeded, and finely chopped Hatch Chiles *(see Hatch Chile Essentials, page 12)*

2 tablespoons unsalted butter, softened

1 teaspoon baking soda

Grease a large, rimmed baking sheet and set it aside.

In a heavy 2-quart saucepan set over medium heat, bring the sugar, corn syrup, salt, and ¼ cup of water to a boil. Stir until the sugar is dissolved, then add the peanuts and stir to coat. Continue cooking, stirring frequently, until the temperature reaches 300°F on a candy thermometer, or a small amount of the mixture separates into hard brittle threads when dropped into very cold water.

Remove the peanut mixture from the heat and immediately stir in the butter, chiles, and baking soda. Pour onto the prepared baking sheet right away. Use 2 forks to lift and stretch the peanut mixture into a rectangle about 12 by 15 inches. Cool the brittle thoroughly. Snap into pieces.

Hatch Chocolate Chip Cookies

makes about 4 dozen cookies

8 ounces (2 sticks) unsalted butter, softened

1 cup granulated sugar

1 cup packed brown sugar

2 eggs

2 teaspoons vanilla extract

3 cups all-purpose flour

1 teaspoon baking soda

½ teaspoon salt

2 cups semisweet chocolate chips

2 Hatch Chiles, roasted, peeled, stemmed, seeded, and finely chopped *(see Hatch Chile Essentials, page 12)*

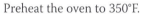

Preheat the oven to 350°F.

Use a handheld mixer or stand mixer to cream together the butter and sugars until smooth. Beat in the eggs one at a time, then stir in the vanilla. Stir in the flour, baking soda, and salt, then mix in the chocolate chips and chiles. Drop the dough by large spoonfuls onto ungreased baking sheets. Bake until the cookies begin to brown, about 10 minutes. Cool on a wire rack.

Easy Hatch Chile Devil's Food Cookies

makes about 50 cookies

1 (15.25-ounce) box Devil's Food Cake Mix

2 teaspoons Melissa's Hatch Chile Powder

8 ounces (2 sticks) unsalted butter, melted

Preheat the oven to 350°F. Line 2 large baking sheets with parchment paper.

Whisk together the cake mix and the chile powder in a mixing bowl. Add the melted butter and mix to form a dough.

Drop the dough onto the parchment-lined baking sheet by teaspoon-size balls, spacing them ½ inch apart. Bake 12 minutes. Use a spatula to transfer the cookies to a wire rack to cool.

Note: *A very light cookie with a subtle kick.*

Hatch Chile-Infused Tequila

makes 2 cups

8 Hatch Chiles, roasted, peeled, stemmed, and seeded *(see Hatch Chile Essentials, page 12)*

2 cups good-quality white tequila

Combine the chiles and the tequila in a 1-quart jar with a tight-fitting lid. Cover the jar tightly and set it in a cool dark cupboard for at least 5 days. Strain the tequila before using. Be sure to label the jar!

Note: *You will notice that the chiles give up some of their color to the tequila. Use the infused tequila to make a Spicy Margarita (page 171), a Hatch Bloody Mary (below), or Tequila shooters.*

Hatch Bloody Mary

makes 1 drink

¼ cup Hatch Chile-Infused Tequila *(page 168)*

6 tablespoons tomato juice

1 tablespoon freshly squeezed lemon juice

2 dashes Worcestershire sauce

Celery stalk, for garnish

Lime wedge, for garnish

Combine the tequila, juices, and Worcestershire sauce in an 8-ounce glass. Stir well. Add ice and garnish with the celery stalk and lime wedge.

Chilled Raspberry *and* Chile Soup

~~~ *makes 4 servings* ~~~

4 cups fresh raspberries

1 ripe banana

1 cup freshly squeezed orange juice

1 Hatch Chile, roasted, peeled, stemmed, seeded, and chopped
(see Hatch Chile Essentials, page 12)

1 cup plain yogurt

2 tablespoons Melissa's Organic Blue Agave Syrup

In a blender, whip all of the ingredients until smooth. Refrigerate the soup for at least 1 hour before serving in small bowls.

Note: *This is a great finish for a meal on a hot summer day.*

Spicy Ice Cubes
and Ginger Ale

~~~~~~~~~~~~~~~~~ *makes 5 (6-ounce) drinks* ~~~~~~~~~~~~~~~~~

6 cups bottled water

1 liter ginger ale

2 Hatch Chiles, roasted, peeled, stemmed, seeded, and coarsely chopped *(see Hatch Chile Essentials, page 12)*

Combine the water and the Hatch Chiles in a blender and blend until the chiles are fully incorporated, then let the chile water sit for 3 to 5 minutes. Skim off any froth that rises to the surface, then pour the chile water into ice cube trays and freeze.

To serve, divide the spicy ice cubes among 5 glasses (2 to 3 cubes each), then fill each glass with ginger ale.

Note: *As the ice cubes melt, the drinks will become spicier.*

Spicy Margarita

makes 1 drink

Kosher salt, for rim of glass

Ice

3 tablespoons Hatch Chile-Infused Tequila *(page 168)*

1 lime, halved

1 tablespoon Triple Sec

1 teaspoon Melissa's Organic Blue Agave Syrup

Spread a thin layer of kosher salt in a shallow dish. Use the cut halves of the lime to moisten the rim of a drinking glass. Set the lime halves aside. Dip the rim of the glass in the salt. Fill the glass with ice, then add the tequila. Squeeze 2 tablespoons of lime juice into the glass, then add the Triple Sec and agave syrup. Stir the mixture a few times to thoroughly mix and chill the ingredients.

Spicy Vanilla Milkshake

makes 4 to 6 shakes

5 cups vanilla ice cream

3 cups whole milk

2 Hatch Chiles, roasted, peeled, stemmed, seeded, and coarsely chopped *(see Hatch Chile Essentials, page 12)*

In blender, combine the ice cream, milk, and chiles. Blend until mixture is smooth and frothy. Pour into glasses and serve.

Index